BLENDED FAMILIES

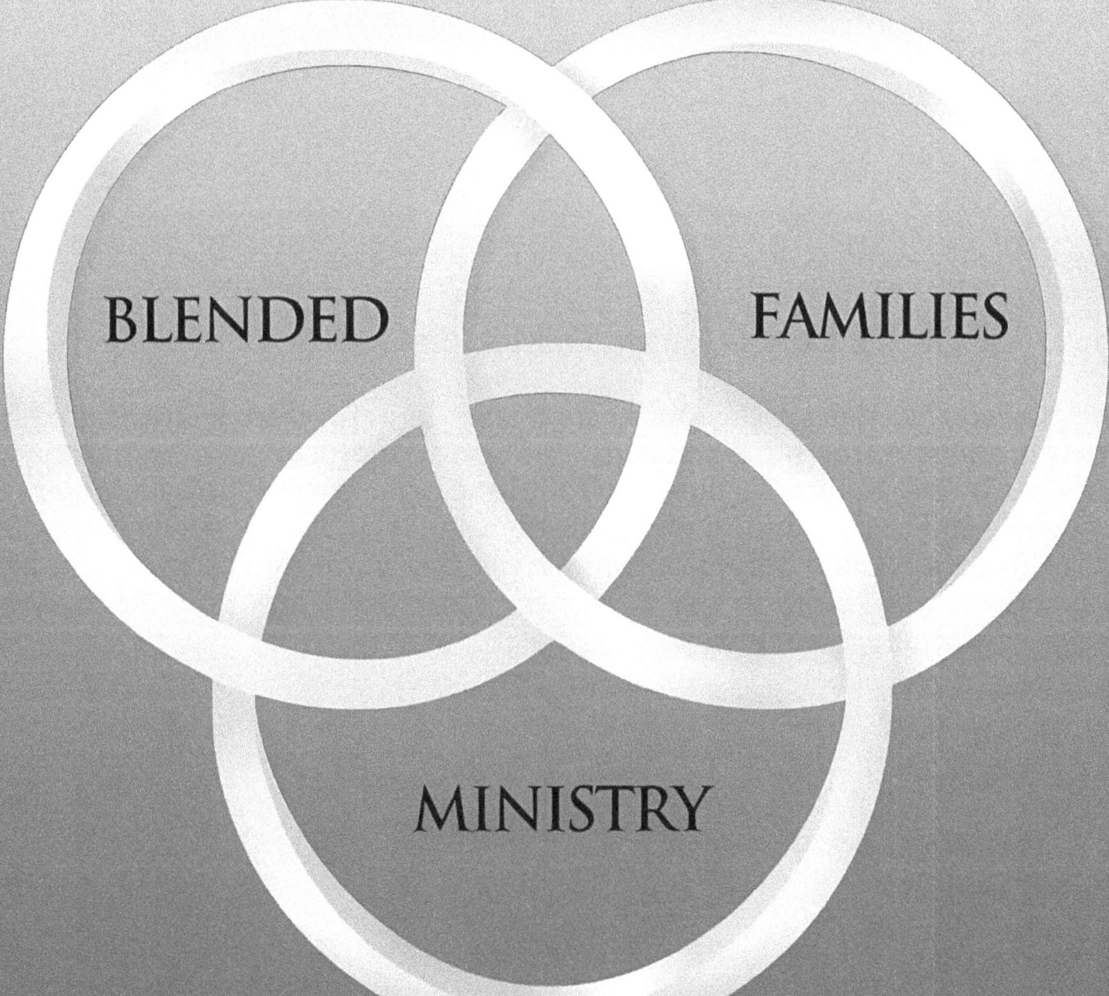

BLENDED   FAMILIES

MINISTRY

Dr. Larry D, Snapp, D. Min. PNC

Dr. Carol A. Snapp, D. Min. PNC

ARPress

ARPress
45 Dan Road Suite 5
Canton MA 02021

Hotline: 1(888) 821-0229
Fax: 1(508) 545-7580

Ordering Information:

Quantity sales. Special discounts are available on quantity purchases by corporations, associations, and others. For details, contact the publisher at the address above.

Printed in the United States of America.

ISBN-13:   Softcover   979-8-89676-104-4
            eBook   979-8-89676-103-7

Library of Congress Control Number: 2024925448

Table of Contents

FORWARD

This curriculum is based on scripture taken from the King James Version of the Holy Bible. It has been written as a guide for those that have remarried or plan to remarry due to divorce or the loss of a spouse.

The principles outlined in this study will help you learn how to put a Godly marriage together where one did not exist before. Our desire is to help you first recognize and then deal with many of the pitfalls found in marriage in general and remarriage in particular.

We will take you through scripture and follow the road map God laid out for marriage in the beginning. We will start the study by laying the foundation for what a Godly marriage should be. From there, we will work on how to deal with the many obstacles and traps that couples often run into.

Some of the topics we will deal with include the following: baggage of past failed marriages, remarriage after divorce, remarriage after the death of a spouse, geographical, age, religious and racial cultural differences, in-law issues and step-parenting and single-parenting skills.

God has put the desire in our hearts to create this curriculum as a way to put His values back into homes and families. We are stepping out in faith based on 2nd Timothy 2:2 "And the things that thou hast heard of me among many witnesses, the same commit thou to faithful men, who shall be able to teach others also."

We hope to reach one home, one man, one woman or even one child at a time, teaching them God's plan for marriage. As they are taught, we pray they also will be able to reach other family members and friends. We also share God's vision to have this teaching spread like a virus. Only this virus won't make you sick. It will help heal you.

We hope this teaching helps you learn so you in turn can teach in your home, your group or your church.

ACKNOWLEDGEMENTS

First and foremost, we would like to thank God for His vision and direction to develop a curriculum for blended families. With a growing number of families being the result of remarriage, there is a need for education on how best to bring "yours, mine and ours" together in a Godly way. Obviously, God hates divorce, but since we live in a fallen world, divorce is a fact of life. We pray that this curriculum will help some of those remarriages become the covenant marriages that God desires and the cycle of divorce will end.

Thank you to Pastors Tommy and Luke Barnett who consistently encouraged us to step up to the plate and reach for the next level of service for the Kingdom of God. Thanks also for providing a great church home environment for us to grow and mature in our relationship with the Lord Jesus Christ. We always look forward to the smiles and hugs we get after each service. Seeing what the Lord is doing through both of you keeps the fire alive in us to strive to find ways to do more. This curriculum is in large part due to the inspiration we have received from you both.

Thank you to Dr. Leo and Molly Godzich for all the training and mentoring we have received. Thanks to their ministry, the National Association of Marriage Enhancement (NAME), our own marriage was restored in 2003. Through their teaching we were able to learn what a Godly marriage should be. God's grace and mercy enabled us to get through our many trials and tribulations. Through the test of fire, we gained much understanding and wisdom about God's plan for marriage. Thank you also for your continued confidence in our ability to teach. Thanks for the opportunities to lead small home group studies and teach workshops at Pastor's School and your International Marriage Conferences (IMCs). We are truly honored to be able to host so many NAME functions in our home.

A very special thank you goes to Pastors Arnold and Gwen Tackett for all the love, time and tears that they shared with us as they took us hand-in-hand through our marriage trials and tribulations. Thank you for planting the seed that eventually grew into the desire to counsel others. It totally changed the course of our lives. Thanks for helping us "Get it." We will forever be joined at the heart even though we are not currently joined at the hip. The Lord definitely has a reason for the four of us coming together. It's still unfolding, but we know it's going to be awesome!

Thanks also to Drs. Richard and Karen Drake whose faith, guidance, support and encouragement helped us complete this project. When the four of us met at our first Phoenix University of Theology graduation there seemed to be a very special bond created. We greatly appreciate your friendship and trust and we are looking forward to discovering what kind of adventure the Lord has in store for all of us.

Finally, we would like to thank all the couples we have had the privilege to counsel over the years who keep proving to us that the Biblical principles outlined in this study are true. When they are applied day-by-day, they work!

Before We Begin

Do you understand the difference between a purchase and a gift? A purchase is something you get through the sacrifice of your own resources. A gift is something you get through the sacrifice of someone else's resources. A gift is something you can't earn or buy. It is something you can only receive through someone else's grace.

At this time, we want to ask you the question requiring the most important answer of your life. If you were to die today, where would you end up? If you do not know absolutely, beyond a shadow of a doubt that you are 100% sure you would spend eternity in Heaven with Jesus, now is the time to make sure.

Salvation is a gift from God. You can't earn it. You have to receive it in faith that it is yours and yours alone. Like a birthday or Christmas gift with your name on it, it's not really yours until you accept the box, open it and take out the gift. Just because you know someone with a similar gift, it doesn't benefit you in any way.

Father God so loved the world that he gave His only begotten son, Jesus Christ to be the sacrifice for the sins of the world. Jesus is the only way to spend eternity in the presence of God.

John 3:16 -

"For God so loved the world, that he gave his only begotten Son, that whosoever believeth in him should not perish, but have everlasting life. "

John 14:6 -

"Jesus saith unto him, I am the way, the truth, and the life: no man cometh unto the Father, but by me."

If you're ready to accept Jesus as your savior you will need to confess your sins and by faith accept His promise to forgive those sins. Then you will need to ask Him to become your Lord and Savior. The following prayer, said out loud, will gain you entrance into the Kingdom of God. You will then become a son or daughter of the King of Kings. Praise the Lord, Amen.

"Dear Heavenly Father, I confess that I have sinned against You. My sins have separated me from You. I am truly sorry, and now I want to repent from my past sinful life toward You. Please forgive me. Father, I believe that your son, Jesus Christ died on a cross for my sins and was resurrected from the dead in three days. He is alive, and He hears my prayers. I'm asking You, Jesus, to become the Lord of my life. Please rule and reign in my heart from this day forward. I am a new creation in You. Please send your Holy Spirit to help me obey You, and to do Your will for the rest of my life. In Jesus' name I pray, Amen."

Chapter 1

What is a Godly Marriage?

This course of study begins by establishing a solid foundation for what a Godly marriage is. This can be applied to any marriage, whether it's a first marriage or a remarriage. Once the foundation is set, we'll delve into the many situations that blended families find themselves dealing with. In today's world, more and more families are being created out of previous marriages that have failed. In order to successfully blend multiple families together you need to know what God intended for marriage in the beginning.

Take a look at what the Scriptures tell us about the establishment of the institution of marriage. Marriage is the first institution created by God.

The institution of marriage begins

Genesis 1:26-28

"26 And God said, Let us make man in our image, after our likeness: and let them have dominion over the fish of the sea, and over the fowl of the air, and over the cattle, and over all the earth, and over every creeping thing that creepeth upon the earth. 27 So God created man in his own image, in the image of God created he him; male and female created he them. 28 And God blessed them, and God said unto them, Be fruitful, and multiply, and replenish the earth, and subdue it: and have dominion over the fish of the sea, and over the fowl of the air, and over every living thing that moveth upon the earth."

Looking at verses 26 through 28, you see that God created man in His own image, both male and female. He blessed them and told them to reproduce, subdue the earth and take dominion over every living thing. It's clear that man and woman were created with a specific purpose in mind. It's also important to keep in mind that God created you in His image. Just knowing you are created in the image of God is the beginning of being able to understand why you are here and what you are supposed to do. More detail will be presented shortly about the differences in your roles and how that applies to your marriage.

Genesis 2:7

"And the LORD God formed man of the dust of the ground, and breathed into his nostrils the breath of life; and man became a living soul."

Genesis 2:18-25

"18 And the LORD God said, It is not good that the man should be alone; I will make him a help meet for him. 19 And out of the ground the LORD God formed every beast of the field, and every fowl of the air; and brought them unto Adam to see what he would call them: and whatsoever Adam called every living creature, that was the name thereof. 20 And Adam gave names to all cattle, and to the fowl of the air, and to every beast of the field; but for Adam there was not found a help meet for him. 21 And the LORD God caused a deep sleep to fall upon Adam, and he slept; and he took one of his ribs, and closed up the flesh instead thereof. 22 And the rib, which the LORD God had taken from man, made he a woman, and brought her unto the man. 23 And Adam said, This is now bone of my bones, and flesh of my flesh: she shall be called Woman, because she was taken out of Man. 24 Therefore shall a man leave his father and his mother, and shall cleave unto his wife: and they shall be one flesh. 25 And they were both naked, the man and his wife, and were not ashamed."

In Genesis 2:18-25 you see that God did not create man and woman at the same time or from the same ingredients. He created Adam out of the dust of the Earth and it wasn't until after Adam had seen and named every living creature that God pronounced it was not good for man to be alone.

This is a very significant point. God determined that man needed someone else comparable to him. You see that God created Eve to be a "help meet" (help mate) for him. Next you see that God created Eve not from the dust of the ground where she would be a separate creation, but from a rib bone of Adam. Eve was created out of Adam's side. She was not created from his head where she would be neither over him nor from his feet where she would be beneath him. She was created to come along side Adam as his partner. She was created to be there to help Adam fulfill the Will of God.

Adam was created first in the full image of God. But when God determined that Adam needed a companion, He put Adam to sleep and then He removed one of Adam's ribs and created a separate female being. He then presented this female being to Adam to name just as he named all the other creatures. Adam named her "Woman" because she was taken "out of Man". This is when God established the institution of marriage. You see in Genesis. 2:24-25 that God is referring to "the man and his wife". Another very significant point is that in verse 24 you see that a man is to leave his father and mother and cleave (be faithful) to his wife thus becoming one flesh.

Recognizing that Adam and Eve were originally "one flesh", you can see that God intended for them to remain one flesh. It's interesting to note that he also warned about potential problems with in-laws even though Adam and Eve only had Father God as their "parent". You will spend much more time with in-law issues in a later chapter. You should also note that God provided the wife that He wanted Adam to have. God needs to be involved in the search for a wife so that a man gets the right one.

God's order in marriage

1 Corinthians 11:2-3

"2 Now I praise you, brethren, that ye remember me in all things, and keep the ordinances, as I delivered them to you. 3 But I would have you know, that the head of every man is Christ; and the head of the woman is the man; and the head of Christ is God."

Within the institution of marriage, God established a certain vertical relationship. As we see in 1 Corinthians 11: 3, Christ is the head of every man; man is the head of the woman; and God the Father is the head of Christ. Anytime this order is out of alignment, there will be all sorts of contentions and strife. It's imperative that in a Godly marriage that Christ is the head of every man. The man's role is to be the Prophet and Priest in his home. Let's look at Ephesians 5 below."

Ephesians 5:21-33

"21 Submitting yourselves one to another in the fear of God. 22 Wives, submit yourselves unto your own husbands, as unto the Lord. 23 For the husband is the head of the wife, even as Christ is the head of the church: and he is the saviour of the body. 24 Therefore as the church is subject unto Christ, so let the wives be to their own husbands in every thing. 25 Husbands, love your wives, even as Christ also loved the church, and gave himself for it; 26 That he might sanctify and cleanse it with the washing of water by the word, 27 That he might present it to himself a glorious church, not having spot, or wrinkle, or any such thing; but that it should be holy and without blemish. 28 So ought men to love their wives as their own bodies. He that loveth his wife loveth himself. 29 For no man ever yet hated his own flesh; but nourisheth and cherisheth it, even as the Lord the church: 30 For we are members of his body, of his flesh, and of his bones. 31 For this cause shall a man leave his father and mother, and shall be joined unto his wife, and they two shall be one flesh. 32 This is a great mystery: but I speak concerning

Christ and the church. 33 Nevertheless let every one of you in particular so love his wife even as himself; and the wife see that she reverence her husband."

It's very clear that husbands are to be the head of their wife AS Christ is the head of the church (which is His bride). As it states in verse 24, the church is subject to Christ, therefore let the wives be subject to their own husbands in everything. This scripture goes back to the book of Genesis chapter 3 that relates the story of Eve being deceived by the serpent and Adam also taking a bite of the forbidden apple. You see below where God is putting a curse directly on Eve. Besides pain in childbirth, her desire will be for her husband but he will be her master. God does not put a curse on Adam, but he does curse the ground so that now Adam will have to toil to make a living from it.

Genesis 3:16-23

"16 Then he said to the woman, "You will bear children with intense pain and suffering. And though your desire will be for your husband, he will be your master."

"17 And to Adam he said, "Because you listened to your wife and ate the fruit I told you not to eat, I have placed a curse on the ground. All your life you will struggle to scratch a living from it. 18 It will grow thorns and thistles for you, though you will eat of its grains. 19 All your life you will sweat to produce food, until your dying day. Then you will return to the ground from which you came. For you were made from dust, and to the dust you will return."

"20 Then Adam named his wife Eve, because she would be the mother of all people everywhere. 21 And the LORD God made clothing from animal skins for Adam and his wife."

"22 Then the LORD God said, "The people have become as we are, knowing everything, both good and evil. What if they eat the fruit of the tree of life? Then they will live forever!" 23 So the LORD God banished Adam and his wife"

What you find in verse 21 is that God made clothing for Adam and Eve out of animal skins. When they had sinned and became aware that they were naked, they tried to use fig leaves to cover themselves. God sacrificed some animals so that Adam and Eve's sin could be covered. You see that God requires blood to be shed as a sacrifice for sin as a preview of Christ shedding his blood on the cross for the sins of mankind.

In a Godly marriage, you need to understand that both of you are sinners. No matter where you are in your walk with God, you must put your full faith and trust in the Lord and not in your spouse. Your spouse is to be seen as a gift from God. Your spouse will let you down sooner or later and you are to remember that you are there as a partner. You are to be there to pick each other up when the other one falls. Your spouse is not your enemy, but rather your partner in a fight against a common enemy – the Devil.

Here's a diagram which represents the priority order of relationships found in a marriage.

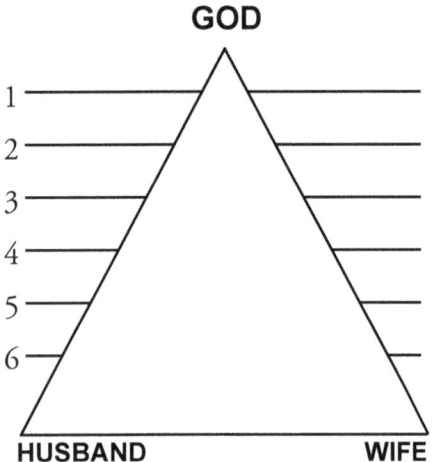

In picture from, a triangle is typically used to represent the priority of relationships as they should be in a Godly marriange. (The "Priority Pyramid")

1. Each spouse's ETERNAL relationship with GOD

2. The covenent FOR LIFE marriage relationship

3. The parental STEPWARDSHIP PERIOD raising God's children (approximately 18-25 years)

4. The relationship with other family and friends FOR A SEASON

5. The relationship with your emplyoer or business FOR A SEASON

6. The relationship with your ministry. Your first ministry should be your spouse and then your immediate family.

God is to be the most important relationship. It's eternal. This is also called the vertical relationship. Each spouse needs to constantly be working on this relationship. When this is in good order, the next relationship (the marriage or horizontal relationship) works best. The marriage is to be a blood covenant, not a contract nor a commitment. A blood covenant is one entered into with your spouse before God and can only be terminated by death. It is written in Malachi 2:16 that God hates divorce, so your goal should be to honor your covenant you have made before God and with your spouse.

Your children come next in the list of priorities. You do not own them. You are to be good stewards of God's children and to teach them for a period of time and then let them go to create their own families. When they are taught well, they will be able to function well on their own.

After your children comes the relationship with your extended family members and friends. You can't pick your relatives so, frequently, God will use them to test your Christian walk. Friends are often only for a season. Some seasons are short while others are life long. You have to listen to the prompting of the Holy Spirit as to when a season is over.

Understand that God has a purpose for each person that He brings into your life. That purpose may be for you to learn from them or you might be the one chosen to teach them.

Next on the priority list is the relationship with your employer. You're to have an abundant life, but you need to keep your job in perspective and not turn it into an idol.

The same goes with your ministry. Serving God is a great calling, but God still wants your home to be in order before you try to do any ministry work. Your spouse and your family are a higher priority ministry than any other ministry.

Be imitators of Christ

Finally, to get the most out of your marriage, be imitators of Christ. Get to know Him intimately. Spend time praying with your spouse on a daily basis. Prayer creates intimacy in three areas: the one to whom you pray, the one with whom you pray and the one(s) for whom you pray. When you exercise God's Grace and

Mercy with your spouse you can cover a multitude of sins that occur in your marriage. Like Christ – let him who is without sin cast the first stone.

Give up your right to be offended. Remember what Christ said as He was dying on the cross – "Father, forgive them, for they know not what they do." He was innocent yet was able to forgive those who were killing Him because He knew they really didn't understand the big picture. How can you as a sinner stand and accuse your spouse of being a sinner without being judged yourself?

Marriage Fundamentals

- Man was created from dust with a need for a relationship.

- Woman was created from man to fill man's need for a relationship.

- Man is to cleave (be faithful) to that wife and become one flesh with her.

- Marriage is a blood covenant - not a contract or commitment.

- God has established an order of priorities for marriage and family

- Pray together daily

- Give up your right to be offended and be quick to extend forgiveness.

BLENDED FAMILIES – DISCUSSION TOPICS – LESSON 1 – What is a Godly Marriage?

- What is the significance in the difference of what God used to create man and woman?

- What is God's chain of command in marriage?

- What is the significance in the difference of what God commanded husbands and wives to do in Ephesians 5:33?

- Describe the Priority Pyramid and the reasons why it is in the order it is.

- Describe the three areas in which intimacy is affected by prayer.

- Why is it important to give up your right to be offended?

Chapter 2

What is a Blended Family?

There are many types of blended families. Technically speaking, a blended family is simply two unrelated families brought together in marriage. The most common blended family is one where two existing families are brought together through remarriage after a divorce or death of a spouse. Other blended family situations are created when spouses from different cultures choose to marry. Different cultures include countries of origin, race, religion and even different parts of the same country. Even a first marriage is a blending of two different families – just with less baggage.

Each type brings with it its own unique challenges. This lesson addresses each type and deals with the issues that frequently present themselves when two diverse families choose to blend together.

As mentioned in the first lesson, Malachi 2:16 tells us that God hates divorce. But since mankind lives in a fallen world, there are many marriages today that are terminated via the law. In Matthew 19:8 it is written, "He said to them, "Moses, because of the hardness of your hearts, permitted you to divorce your wives, but from the beginning it was not so.

In this lesson, you'll look at the two most common types of blended families (at least in the US) – one being created from two existing divorced families and one where a marriage involves a family where at least one of the spouses is a widow or widower.

Remarriage after divorce

One of the most important issues to address in this situation is the root cause for failure of the previous marriage. To use an agricultural example – you don't want to bring weeds from your old pasture into your new pasture. When the problems that resulted in the death of the previous marriage are not dealt with, they will most certainly reappear in the new marriage.

One of the greatest blessings through God's Grace is the chance to receive forgiveness for your sins and become a new creation in Christ. God allows do-overs! He would prefer we do it right the first time since He has given us clear boundaries, but He is a forgiving and longsuffering God who loves us unconditionally. God desires obedience rather than sacrifice.

Marriage is hard enough when it's just two people trying to blend themselves into that one flesh that God desires. Satan hates marriage as much as God hates divorce. So the Enemy is constantly going to be trying to tear apart what God put together.

If there has been adultery, addictive behaviors or abuse of any kind in a previous marriage, it creates trust issues in the new marriage. Trust is difficult to rebuild once it has been broken. It has to be earned over time. It can't be demanded. Selfishness is another very common cause of divorce that is normally carried over to subsequent marriages. Financial problems are also a leading cause of divorce that usually impacts future marriages.

These problems need to be dealt with. If adultery was the cause of divorce in the previous marriage, then there has to be some accountability for a period of time that will satisfy the spouse's need for security and trust. Accountability should be between the person who committed adultery and a Godly 3rd party of the same gender. The spouse should not be the accountability partner because a spouse should not have to act or feel like they are the adultery police.

Addictions, such as sex, drugs or alcohol, frequently need special and/or professional help. However, all things are possible with God and through Christ you can do all things. Once a person gives their life to Christ, He can help them overcome these addictions. Once again, you are a new creation and the old man has died. Through the renewing of your mind through the washing of the Word of God, you can become what God created you to be.

If one spouse in a new marriage has come from an abusive marriage or was abused as a child, forgiveness is key. Otherwise, the fear and anger created in the past will destroy the intimacy that God desires for a husband and wife. Children of abuse have a very difficult time understanding what a Heavenly Father is like when their own father was abusive. There's no way to relate to unconditional love and forgiveness when all you ever received has been physical, verbal, mental or sexual abuse. In cases of abuse, counseling can be very helpful, as well as finding small group Bible studies to be part of. It's important to learn who you are in Christ rather than believing all the lies you've been told in the past. Past abuses can take significant time to heal through counseling and the spouse of one that has been abused has to have a great deal of patience and grace.

What is being attempted here is to help you deal with the old baggage from the previous marriage. This lesson will also provide a Christian road map to help you keep your new marriage on the right track going forward as God intended for all marriages.

The biggest challenge in remarriage is when there are children involved – even more so when each spouse has children from the previous marriage. Each spouse tends to favor their own kids over the other spouse's children. Besides "yours" and/or "mine", there are special challenges when there is "ours" added into the mix.

Reflecting back on the "Priority Pyramid" in lesson 1, you need to focus on the order of priorities. When it comes to blending two existing families, it's vital for the husband and wife to elevate their marital relationship above the children. Many counseling sessions have been with couples that have had major problems in their marital relationship because one spouse regards their own children from the previous marriage higher than their spouse.

One of the most important purposes of a husband and wife is teaching their children about God. You read in Proverbs 22:6 "Train up a child in the way he should go: and when he is old, he will not depart from it." The values you teach your children will be carried forward in their home and their children's home. God is a generational God and he wants godly offspring. Children grow up so quickly, but the memories (good or bad) linger on. The best thing a father can do for his children is to love the mother of his children. In a blended family, "yours, mine and ours" needs to become only "ours". A husband loves his wife's children because he loves their mother and they are a part of her. Likewise, a wife loves her husband's children because she loves him and they are part of him.

Children need to see that Mom and Dad are united in all that they do. The children need to see them as that one-flesh that God desires in a marital union. This provides a great example for the children of a Godly marriage so that when they get married, they will know what to do. Unfortunately, what happens in many cases is that the children will rebel and will constantly and deliberately pit one spouse against the other.

As you saw in lesson 1, God told Adam and Eve to leave and cleave because he knew there would be problems with in-laws. When one spouse speaks poorly about their own spouse to their Mother or Father, it opens the relationship up for the Enemy to get in and create havoc. In "the olden days", it was customary for a prospective groom to ask the father of the bride for permission to marry his daughter. This rarely happens today. Hence, many extended families have prejudices that create stumbling blocks for the couple that marries. It's very common for one family to feel that the person marrying their child is not good enough and they frequently try to "move in" and control many things that happen in the new marriage. Again, this is why the marriage relationship needs to be elevated to 2nd place only to the individual relationship with God.

You are to breathe life into your marriage and family with your words. Too many times, you are in the flesh and instead you speak death. Ist Corinthians 13 tells you that love covers all sins. Therefore, you should cover your mate's sin especially with in-laws rather than expose them. That does not mean that you have to approve of the sin. God loves the sinner but hates the sin. Sin will always be exposed eventually if it is left to continue unchecked. Covering the sin means exposing it to God where it can be dealt with, but not the whole family where judgment and condemnation can arise. Never give your parents ammunition to use against your spouse. Don't forget that you are one flesh and whatever you do to your spouse that hurts them, ultimately hurts yourself.

Make time to plan things with your spouse. Work at being united in all things such as goals, finances, disciplinary actions, family nights and events. Talk to one another and to the children. Take time with each other and listen to each other and be silent to hear what God is telling you.

Remarriage after the death of a spouse

Remarriage after losing a spouse is a very different spiritual situation than a remarriage after divorce. A widow or widower is spiritually free from the original blood covenant that they entered into with God and is now free to remarry and enter into a new covenant. When it comes to blending two families however, most of what was described above applies here as well (children and in-laws) so this lesson will deal primarily with the differences.

Where divorce is the result of at least one of two people being hard-hearted and failing to apply the Word of God appropriately, the loss of a spouse does not carry with it the same types of baggage. Generally speaking, you're not dealing with the same unhealthy behavior characteristics. There is still the loss of a loved one to grieve which takes a length of time only known to the one that lost the spouse. In 2nd Corinthians 6:14, we are told "Be ye not unequally yoked together with unbelievers: for what fellowship hath righteousness with unrighteousness? and what communion hath light with darkness?". It's especially important when a spouse has died that when you are ready to remarry, that you find a partner who is also a follower of Christ. For the purposes of this lesson, assume that is the case.

In addition to the "normal" problems associated with blending two different families already mentioned above, one of the biggest problems is that the new spouse often has a hard time measuring up to the old spouse. It's kind of like a pair of shoes. The old pair was very comfortable. The new pair sometimes will put a blister on your heel until you get them broken in. The blister will heal and eventually the new pair becomes another old pair and feels "just right". You don't throw out the new pair just because you got a blister. You endure through the pain at the beginning because you know that it will feel good in time. God's Grace is sufficient for all your needs. 2nd Corinthians 12:9 tells us, "And he said unto me, My grace is sufficient for thee: for my strength is made perfect in weakness. Most gladly therefore will I rather glory in my infirmities, that the power of Christ may rest upon me."

In a "good marriage", after the loss, it is common for the irritations of the departed spouse that were put up with over the years to be diminished over time. This creates a situation where the departed starts to be idolized to some extent and only the good memories retained. If it was a marriage that was simply being endured, maybe it's just good riddance and you will be much happier with your new spouse. Everything discussed to this point still applies.

It's important for the new spouse to be sensitive to the situation and understand the grieving process. They must have grace and patience with the one who lost their previous spouse and understand that there will probably be times when there is a comparison made. Likewise, it is important that the spouse that had the loss be keenly aware that they are no longer married to the departed and their current spouse is a totally new and different person. It would be wise for this couple to spend time in the beginning of their relationship talking about their past relationships (if any) to aid in the other spouse's understanding of where they are coming from.

Celebrate your differences; don't look at them as points of contention. Find ways to learn about and understand those differences. God puts two people together so that they can be greater as a couple than either one of them could ever be alone. By default, this means that one spouse will have gifts in areas that the other does not. Be willing to give credence to the partner with the gifting in the various areas such as finances, hospitality or organization. Since you are to be functioning as one flesh, it shouldn't matter who does what as long as the one that has the better gift for the task is the one doing it.

God made you for His pleasure and He desires your obedience rather than your sacrifice. You can only do this through His Holy Spirit living in you. For the best chance of success when blending two families, do it God's way. A three-stranded rope is not easily broken.

Keep the order of priorities as described in the "Priority Pyramid" example in lesson 1.

BLENDED FAMILIES – DISCUSSION TOPICS – LESSON 2 – What is a Blended Family?

- Discuss what variety of blended family you are.

- Discuss why marriage can be so difficult in general and remarriage in particular.

- What is one of the most important functions of a husband and wife?

- Explain why it is critical to conform to the Priority Pyramid in a Blended Family with children.

- From a spiritual perspective, what is the major difference between a remarriage after divorce and the remarriage after the loss of a spouse?

- Discuss how God's Grace needs to be walked out after a widow or widower remarries.

Chapter 3

Celebrate the Differences

There are two basic areas to touch on in this lesson. In the first area, the individual differences between the husband and the wife will be dealt with. In the second, the differences that come into play with the extended family will be dealt with. These differences include: nationalities, cultures, races, religions, age, geographic regions, etc.

For this lesson, consider any marriage as the creation of a blended family. The topics discussed will apply just as much to the blending of two extended families through a first marriage as it will for the blending of two (or more) families which have step-parents involved.

Some of you have never been out of the country and have not been exposed to cultures other than the American culture. Others grew up somewhere outside the United States and have experienced a very different way of life. Every country and culture influences your own prejudices as you grow into adulthood.

As you go through life as a child, you learn your own family's traditions and their way of doing things. These things become the "normal" that you compare everything else to as you grow older. These things could be good or bad. If you feel they're good, you would want to duplicate them in your life as an adult. If you feel they were bad, they would be things that you would want to avoid doing when you're an adult and not pass them on in your own family. However, many times these bad things still get passed on in your adult life.

When God brings two people of His choosing together in marriage, He always brings the perfect pair of partners together that will complement each other's abilities and will help each other mature spiritually. God desires that the two, being married, will become one flesh. The goal being that the multiplication of the two parts (1 x 1 = 1) will generate something even greater than either one of the individuals standing alone.

It's similar to magnets. Opposing magnetic forces attract and like forces repel. Would you really want to be married to someone that was exactly like you? Most of you would rather marry someone that would make you stronger rather than weaker. You all have various strengths and weaknesses. When you seek God and ask Him for the spouse that He has created for you, He brings to you a partner with the perfect set of complementary strengths and weaknesses. That way, as a one-flesh couple, you now have a partner that possesses strengths that offset your weaknesses. The weaknesses of the combined pair have been diminished because each partner can do things in which the other isn't especially gifted.

When you marry without first seeking the Will of God, very likely you will not have chosen the partner that God specifically created for you. You will have married for the wrong reason. In this case, it's never too late to create a new covenant and build a new relationship with God. Once each spouse turns their life over to Christ, they will begin a new journey that will bless their marriage and their families. Otherwise, they will face the consequences of failing to wait on God to provide the best mate. God always honors His covenant. You, as a sinner, often break the covenants you make, but God always keeps His. When God is brought in to a marriage as the third strand of the cord, He will honor this covenant. It's not where you've been that God cares about. It's about you figuring out where God wants you to be that matters.

A pre-marital class really helps. It can be a real eye opener, bringing to light the really big differences two people have regarding how to handle money, how many children to have, with whose family to celebrate holidays, how to teach and how to discipline the children. If there are any red flags, take them seriously!

Who's Normal is Normal?

Now it's time to really celebrate and discuss your differences. How do you decide who's "normal" is right for the new blended family? As was mentioned earlier, each person's "normal" is determined by where and the way they were brought up and the many experiences they encountered.

This is where friction often develops in a marriage. Once the honeymoon is over, the conflict between the two different 'normals' starts to become a factor in daily life. The conflicts can be over major differences as well as things that most people would consider insignificant. The Enemy likes to use your differences to create in you the feeling that one of the spouses is right (me) and the other is wrong (you). Different isn't wrong – it's just different. Differences in your pasts when looked at as something to celebrate and discover can make the journey through life together a very exciting adventure. When they are misunderstood and looked at as something to be corrected or feared, it turns life with your spouse into something to be endured rather than enjoyed.

In the majority of counseling sessions, communication is the one factor that couples seem to have the most trouble with. Communication involves a lot more listening than it does talking. You have two ears and one mouth for a reason. You need to spend time with your spouse listening to them describe their normal. Listen to how they feel about the way they were brought up and the many things that they experienced in their life. The better you understand each other's normal, the better you can be at determining their needs and meeting them. Be sure to use God's Word as your base-line when discussing your 'normals'. It will help you see where changes need to be made in your own life to correct erroneous teachings from your past

A large difference in 'normals' can sometimes make the greatest marriage. When there is a large difference in your 'normals', obviously there can be some big obstacles to overcome. The bigger the gap, the greater the need for God to create the bridge that will close it. Have you ever sharpened a knife using a butcher's steel? As you read in Proverbs 27:17:

Proverbs 27:17

"Iron sharpeneth iron; so a man sharpeneth the countenance of his friend."

When iron strikes iron, sometimes sparks fly. Some of the strongest and longest lasting marriages are the ones that have "good" arguments. These couples have learned the art of sharpening one another by making sparks fly once in awhile. These couples have also learned the art of forgiveness. Couples that avoid arguments look like they're OK on the surface, but underneath, the issues are seldom resolved and eventually something blows up and can often be catastrophic.

In your day-to-day life you have many choices to make. You have to choose things such as where to live, what kind of housing, where and how you worship God, transportation options, and choices for your children's food, clothing, music and friends. Agreement between spouses when making these choices creates a powerful environment of teamwork.

Now that you've blended two families into a new one, start making your own new memories for you and all of your children. Create some brand new traditions of your own so they will have something of their own to pass onto their children. Do what you can to distinguish your blended family from either of the previous families. In the effort to create a new family with new traditions, it's important to not speak evil of the ex-spouse when there's been a divorce. It's also inappropriate to speak evil of other extended family members (in-laws). Nothing should be coming out of your mouth that doesn't edify the one you are speaking of.

Ephesians 4:@-32

""29 Let no corrupt communication proceed out of your mouth, but that which is good to the use of edifying, that it may minister grace unto the hearers. 30 And grieve not the Holy Spirit of God, whereby ye are sealed unto the day of redemption. 31 Let all bitterness, and wrath, and anger, and clamor, and evil speaking, be put away from you, with all malice: 32 and be ye kind one to another, tender-hearted, forgiving one another, even as God for Christ's sake hath forgiven you."

Many have vowed at one time or another that they would never become like their parents only to catch themselves quoting what they heard as a child. A blended a family benefits greatly through communicating about your childhood 'normals' in order to reach agreement on guidelines for discipline. For example, your spouse's childhood was too strict or abusive with excessive punishment while yours was too lenient with very little discipline. In this situation, neither normal would make an appropriate role model. Search God's Word to find the right combination for dispensing grace, mercy, discipline and punishment. Pray with each other about this and then make your own list for your home as God leads you. The goal is to be able to reach an agreement as to how to raise godly offspring. You will be powerless without it.

Don't let the differences tear you down. Let them make you stronger and find ways to use them to give your children a well-rounded education – teach them how and where you came from. Use times of discipline to teach your children about the ways of God. When you make mistakes, God uses them as teachable moments in your lives. You should do the same with your own children.

When you have a trial, you are to take it to God together giving prayers of thanksgiving.

Ephesians 5:20

"Giving thanks always for all things unto God and the Father in the name of our Lord Jesus Christ;"

Be silent and listen for what God is trying to teach you. Whatever he tells you to do regarding your situation you must do. He won't give you more than you can handle. Sometimes you feel you've gotten double portions and your plate is overflowing. Instead of complaining about that, thank God for the blessing of not having a plate that's empty. How loudly do people whine even over little things? Remind yourself you are the son or daughter of the King of Kings. Act accordingly.

In-laws or Outlaws?

Blending an extended family can be even more difficult than blending "yours, mine and ours". You have very little control over what your extended family does. You can avoid many problems by showing your in-laws the respect they are due. Take the time to get to know as many of them as possible so you can find something in common with them. Every family has the crazy uncle or someone that seems to be the oddball out there on the fringe of reality.

Blending the extended family can bring to light a lot of issues surrounding those cultural differences described at the beginning of this lesson. You will have in-laws that will want to dictate their own ideals and normals into your blended family. Holidays can be big problem areas. Whose traditions are you going to observe? Who has the better food?

Religious, racial and all sorts of prejudices surface when you start dealing with your extended family. Romans 2:11 shows us that to God, we are all the same. God doesn't love anyone more than anyone else. Blending a family works best when we share God's viewpoint. You are all His children and He loves you all unconditionally.

Romans 2:11 –

"For there is no respect of persons with God."

There will be many opportunities to be offended by or be offensive to your in-laws. In extreme cases of offense by in-laws, it may be necessary to set boundaries with them. Remember, the marital relationship between you and your spouse needs to be elevated above the relationship with your in-laws. Even the parent/child relationship needs to be a higher priority than the relationship with the in-laws. Being able to deal with offense is a key ingredient to a successful relationship with your in-laws. It's also a key ingredient for a successful relationship with your spouse and your children.

Offenses that occur can be related to what happens in the legal system. If you commit an offense, you can be held responsible for your actions. The person who was offended by you has the legal right to be compensated for any damages that you may have caused. Likewise, you have a legal right to seek damages from someone that offends you.

What God expects from you is to give up your right to be offended and instead, forgive the party that committed the offense. Christ gave up His right to be offended while He was being crucified and prayed "Father, forgive them, for they know not what they do."

Luke 23:34

"Then said Jesus, Father, forgive them; for they know not what they do. And they parted his raiment, and cast lots."

It's not easy, but understand that when people offend you, many times they don't even realize that they are being offensive. In some cases, it's deliberate, but either way, you are still to forgive those that trespass against you.

Matthew 6:14-15 –

"For if ye forgive men their trespasses, your heavenly Father will also forgive you: But if ye forgive not men their trespasses, neither will your Father forgive your trespasses."

You must forgive if you expect to be forgiven. Be quick to say, "I'm sorry." Make the effort to create a peaceful environment at home with your spouse and when you are with your in-laws. Treating your spouse with respect will return you a harvest of respect from them. As a Christian, you are called not only to be a peace keeper, but to be s peace maker.

James 3:18

"And the fruit of righteousness is sown in peace of them that make peace."

BLENDED FAMILIES – DISCUSSION TOPICS – LESSON 3 – Celebrate the Differences

- Discuss how your family traditions influence your idea of "normal".

- How does God create one flesh out of two different people?

- Discuss the consequences of not seeking God's Will in choosing your spouse. How can your marriage be redeemed if that was the case in your current marriage?

- Discuss how Proverbs 27:17 ("iron sharpens iron") applies to working out differences of opinion as to whose "normal" is normal.

- What is the scripture that teaches how to speak about your ex-family members?

- Reflecting on the Priority Pyramid, why could it be necessary to impose boundaries with your in-laws if their actions are creating conflict in your marriage?

Chapter 4

Placement of the Mantle

As an imperfect human being, you can frequently get things out of order compared to the "Priority Pyramid" in Lesson 1 - especially where a blended family is concerned. A very common reason for problems in a blended family is due to a difference of opinion as to who is going to wear the mantle of leadership.

Two families, both used to being led by a single parent are now trying to blend into one family with two parents. Who's going to lead now? This lesson will discuss the mantle of leadership and how it should be worn in a two-parent family according to the plan God set forth in Scripture.

2nd Kings 2:13 -

"He took up also the mantle of Elijah that fell from him, and went back, and stood by the bank of Jordan;"

This verse refers to Elisha picking up the mantle that Elijah threw down as he (Elijah) was being carried off into Heaven in a chariot of fire.

A mantle was the official garment worn by a prophet. The mantle immediately marked a man as a prophet and spokesman of God. It let people know that there had been sacrifice and a commitment to God. A prophet's life was not a life of luxury. The mantle he wore represented a man's gift, his calling by God, and the purpose for which God had called him.

Going back to lesson 1, you saw where God cursed the ground and told Adam he would have to work the land to survive and provide for himself and his wife. God cursed Eve so that (in addition to pain in childbirth) she would want to be equal in leadership to her husband but was told by God that she would have to live in submission to her husband. She was created from Adam to be a helpmate not his supervisor. Having been created from a rib, it was intended for her to be one who would come along side and be a helper and encourager.

Ever since Adam, men have had a natural tendency towards laziness. If given the chance, many men would gladly give up wearing the mantle and the responsibility that goes with it. Women have a natural tendency to want to be in charge. That sounds like a perfect solution to the problem, right? Women want to be in charge and men are usually eager to give up the steering wheel. So, what naturally happens in a marriage is the husband chooses to not wear his mantle and leaves it lying on the floor.

The natural wife feels insecure. She feels a need to pick up the mantle and put it on to regain some sense of security since someone has to be in charge. However, when this situation arises, what naturally happens is that the husband resents his wife when she inevitably tries to become his parole officer. Likewise, the wife resents her husband for putting the responsibility of the family on her shoulders. Eventually, the resentment builds to a level that creates such hostility that divorce seems to be the only answer. The husband needs to accept his roles as prophet, priest and king and the responsibility that goes with them. His purposes are to guide, guard and govern.

Try to visualize this example of wearing the mantle –

A couple is in their best Sunday outfits. The husband has on a very nice, custom-tailored suit and the wife is wearing one of her best designer dresses. All of a sudden, the husband, in his natural state of being, decides his mantle is getting too heavy for him. He takes it off and just drops it on the floor. The wife, in her natural state of being bends down and picks it up and puts it on over her designer dress.

The husband feels more comfortable now that he does not have so much weight on his shoulders. But now, the wife is feeling the extra weight of the mantle that she has picked up. It doesn't look good and doesn't come close to fitting her since it was tailor made for her husband. The shoulders are too wide and the sleeves are too long. It ruins the sleek lines of her designer dress. A wife is to be the glory of her husband but her husband is to be the image and glory of God.

1 Corinthians 11:7 -

"For a man indeed ought not to cover his head, forasmuch as he is the image and glory of God: but the woman is the glory of the man."

Most of you have probably heard the phrase "Behind every great man there is a great woman." A man derives the majority of his self-worth through what he does. Therefore, he needs his wife to be for him and not against him. The average man will only accomplish things in life according to the level of belief his wife has in him. He will invariably live up to her expectations of him. If they are high and she is edifying him, he will strive to meet those expectations. If her expectations are low and she is tearing him down, he will accomplish very little.

A good scriptural reference for this is Proverbs 14:1.

Proverbs 14:1 –

"A wise woman builds her house; a foolish woman tears hers down with her own hands."

If a wife has high expectations but a low level of faith in her husband being able to meet them, both spouses will be disappointed and resentful. If the wife has spent sufficient time getting to know her husband, she will be able to know how to encourage and bless him and he will be able to accomplish much more in life than he would ever have been able to on his own.

As we read Proverbs 12:4 we see a woman can be either of two very different things to her husband. One attribute is highly desirable while the other is like a cancer.

Proverbs 12:4 -

"A virtuous woman is a crown to her husband: but she that maketh ashamed is as rottenness in his bones."

Blending a family, especially after a divorce situation, requires that both the husband and wife be aware of the impact they can have on each other and any children that might be involved. They need to understand the power of their words and their actions towards one another. In many gift shops there is often a sign that says, "If Momma ain't happy, ain't nobody happy." That sounds very similar to Proverbs 21:19.

Proverbs 21:19 –
"It is better to dwell in the wilderness, than with a contentious and an angry woman."

The husband, as mentioned earlier is to be prophet, priest and king. His role as prophet is to speak the Word of God and teach his family what the Word of God says about them and the way they should behave.

His role as priest is to provide the spiritual leadership and covering for his wife and his family. When he is fulfilling his role as priest, it creates an atmosphere of security and comfort for his wife. When she's at ease, the temperature in the home is usually at a comfortable level. When that's not being done, the Enemy has easier access to alter the thermostat and can make the temperature either too hot to handle or frigidly cold.

Men will do almost anything to please a woman when she is encouraging and has positive things to say about him. Wives need to beware that if they are generally tearing down and saying negative things, their husband will be easily tempted by a flattering female. Men especially need to be putting on the full armor of God (see Ephesians 6) to avoid these temptations. Proverbs 5:3-9 has a lot to say regarding this issue –

Proverbs 5:3-9

"3 For the lips of a strange woman drop as a honeycomb, and her mouth is smoother than oil: 4 but her end is bitter as wormwood, sharp as a two-edged sword. 5 Her feet go down to death; her steps take hold on hell. 6 Lest thou shouldest ponder the path of life, her ways are movable, that thou canst not know them. 7 Hear me now therefore, O ye children, and depart not from the words of my mouth. 8 Remove thy way far from her, and come not nigh the door of her house: 9 lest thou give thine honor unto others, and thy years unto the cruel:"

A successful blended family needs to move beyond those natural tendencies of the flesh and move into the supernatural. You need a third party to help you perform in that supernatural realm in order to fulfill your God-intended roles and responsibilities. That third party is Jesus Christ who came to help you live an abundant life. When the husband's relationship with Christ is in good standing, he will speak life and blessings over his wife and family. When the wife's relationship is in good standing, she will understand her role as the multifaceted helper who is there to edify and strengthen her husband and nurture her children. They will both understand that they are there to pick each other up should one fall - not kick them while they are down.

Ecclesiastes 4:12 -

"And if one prevail against him, two shall withstand him; and a threefold cord is not quickly broken."

This scripture gives you a good idea of how important it is for Christ to be in the middle of a marriage. It makes the relationship so much stronger when Christ is at the head of both the husband and the wife. As was mentioned in lesson 2, it's vital that the husband and wife relationship be elevated above the parent/child relationship. When both spouses are spending time in God's Word, praying together daily and listening to what God has to say there will be a high level of intimacy, peace and unity in the relationship. It takes time and effort from each spouse to make a marriage work. Marriage is not a 50%-50% arrangement. It has to be a relationship in which each party gives 100% effort to make it succeed.

When each spouse is living up to their God-given roles and responsibilities, the children see that there is peace and security in the home. They learn about the relationship you are all to have with Christ. They can see that the relationship that Father and Mother have with each other resembles that which Christ has with His bride (the Church) and it sets a great example for them to take into their own life down the road. They will be better prepared to understand God's grace and forgiveness because they will have received both from their earthly father and mother.

One example of how the roles and responsibilities work best in a Christ-centered family can be taken from the world of big business. When we look at a corporation, there is always the Chairman of the Board, the Board members, the Chief Executive Officer (CEO) and the Chief Operations Officer (COO). When we apply this structure to a family we have God being the Chairman of the Board. He is fully responsible for the overall success of the company. He is the ultimate authority in the company and the buck stops with him. He establishes the overriding vision and mission for the company.

The Chairman of the Board gives the husband (CEO) the direction he wants the company to go. The CEO's job is to take the vision from the Chairman and share it with the rest of the company (the family) and get their buy-in. The CEO then communicates daily with the wife (COO) to determine the various tasks that need to be completed to get the job done. It's the COO's responsibility to ensure that the day-to-day tasks get done so that the vision can become a reality. Families that put in the effort to build each other up and accept their roles and responsibilities can create a well-oiled machine that produces great fruit for the Kingdom of God.

BLENDED FAMILIES – DISCUSSION TOPICS – LESSON 4 – Placement of the Mantle

• Discuss the significance of the mantle of leadership in the home.

• Going back to the Garden of Eden, describe the curses God spoke after Adam and Eve sinned. How does that curse manifest itself in today's marriages?

• Discuss how Proverbs 14:1 relates to the wearing of the mantle in a marriage.

• What 3 things make up the husband's role in the home?

• What are two main roles of the wife in the home?

• Based on Ecclesiastes 4:12, what is the significance of the 3-stranded cord?

• Describe the God/Husband/Wife relationship in context of a corporation.

Chapter 5

The Spousal Relationship

When attempting to blend a family, perhaps the greatest cause for difficulty is simply the physical and mental differences between men and women. It should be obvious that due to the physical differences, men and women were created for completely different and very specific purposes. This lesson will focus on the differences in the physical and mental aspects plus the different purposes for which we were created by God. Also touched on in this lesson is why there are problems when you try to, or have to, perform the roles of the other spouse.

First take a quick and simple look at the rules rather than the exceptions regarding the physical differences between men and women.

Genesis 1:28 –

"And God blessed them, and God said unto them, Be fruitful, and multiply, and replenish the earth, and subdue it: and have dominion over the fish of the sea, and over the fowl of the air, and over every living thing that moveth upon the earth."

God told Adam and Eve to be fruitful and multiply and fill the Earth. Men and women were created by God to produce the godly offspring he desires. Men are created to provide the sperm to fertilize the egg produced by the female to create new life. More time will be spent on the sexual relationship later in this lesson. God intended for there to be more to the spousal relationship than just procreation.

Men are created to be fathers and represent the Heavenly Father to his family. This is the highest calling. Fathers are created (as mentioned in an earlier lesson) to guide, guard and govern. It's a father's job to determine the direction the family should take through his intimate relationship with God. As he leads them on their journey through life, he needs to protect them from harm. He needs to protect them spiritually, emotionally and physically. When necessary, he needs to discipline his children as God disciplines His children. A father is to train up his children in the way they should go according to Proverbs 22:6. One of the greatest things a father can do for his children is to love their mother.

Proverbs 22:6 –

"Train up a child in the way he should go: and when he is old, he will not depart from it."

Women are created to be wives and mothers. In addition to being the companion, pillar of support and encouragement and crown of glory for her husband, a mother is created to nourish, comfort and teach her children. Her role is to teach them not only about God, but about life. She needs to transfer the knowledge she has gained throughout her life to her children.

Waffles or Spaghetti?

Men's brains are like waffles. Women's brains are like a plate of spaghetti. This is one way to visualize how big a difference there is in the way men's and women's brains work. Take a look at the scientific reasons why men and women are so different in the way they utilize their mental processes.

During the twelfth to fourteenth week of gestation, a fetus's brain undergoes a chemical bath. A female fetus gets an estrogen based chemical bath that doesn't seem to impact the structure or function of the brain. In males, the bath is testosterone based. Testosterone impacts the level of the neurotransmitter Seratonin in the brain.

As testosterone levels increase, so do the Seratonin levels. As the Seratonin level goes up, so does the rate of neuron firing. It is believed that this chemical bath affects the Corpus Collosum - a band of nerves that connect the two hemispheres of the brain. With fewer bands, it is harder to switch from the Cognitive side of the brain to the Intuitive side. These bands have been found to be noticeably larger in females.

Therefore, women often conclude that men are born brain damaged. Just kidding!

As you just saw, men generally only use one side of their brain at a time. They are created to be logical thinkers. They are created to be more focused on single tasks. That's where the waffle comes into play. Men tend to compartmentalize everything. They work on one task at a time and when they switch to another task, they have to put the previous task back in its little waffle square.

A man is to be in tune with God. He should be getting the visions for the future direction of his family directly from Him. It is his job then to impart that vision to his spouse and family and lead them accordingly. He is to be focused on the task at hand and maintain the forward progress of whatever mission God has prepared for them. For example, in the Old Testament, Joseph was given visions through dreams that he was to lead Mary out of harm's way. Because of the way a man's brain is wired, he normally spends his time thinking either in the present or in the future. This makes it easier for a man to forgive, put hurtful things behind him and move on.

Women are able to use both sides of their brain at the same time. They are created to be relational thinkers. That's where the plate full of spaghetti comes into play. When you look at a plate of spaghetti, all the noodles are tangled up and overlapping. It's hard to determine the beginning and end of any one noodle. Because of the way a woman's brain is wired, she normally spends her time thinking in the present and in the past. This makes it more difficult for her to let go of hurtful things and move on. Being relational, a woman spends more time collecting information about where she's been, who she's talked to and how she got where she is now. It also makes it more difficult for women to forgive and especially to forget than it does for a man.

The difference in the way male and female brains are wired is a common source of miscommunication. Men, if you've ever wondered why your wife frequently brings up things you did in the past, now you know why. Women, now you can understand why it's so hard to get your husband's attention when he's in the middle of some project. Understanding how your spouse's brain works goes a long way towards enabling better communication in the spousal relationship.

The Sexual Relationship

This portion of the lesson starts by looking at:

1st Corinthians 7:1-7

1 Now concerning the things whereof ye wrote unto me: It is good for a man not to touch a woman. 2 Nevertheless, to avoid fornication, let every man have his own wife, and let every woman have her own husband. 3 Let the husband render unto the wife due benevolence: and likewise also the wife unto the husband. 4 The wife hath not power of her own body, but the husband: and likewise also the husband hath not power of his own body, but the wife. 5 Defraud ye not one the other, except it be with consent for a time, that ye may give yourselves to fasting and prayer; and come together again, that Satan tempt you not for your incontinency. 6 But I speak this by permission, and not of commandment. 7 For I would that all men were even as I myself. But every man hath his proper gift of God, one after this manner, and another after that.

What you find here is that the sexual relationship was intended to be only between one husband and one wife. Verse 1 shows you that prior to marriage, a man should not touch a woman. God intended for a man and a women to enter into marriage in a virgin state. Immediately after the wedding ceremony, the new groom and his bride would go off to "the tent" to consummate the marriage. After some time, the two fathers would then check the bed linens for signs of blood. The woman's hymen, when torn, would issue a small amount of blood. This is God's way of showing that a marriage is a blood covenant. Normally, the father of the groom would pay for the wedding, but if they found no issue of blood, the father of the bride would have to reimburse the groom's father.

You also see that a husband and wife are to give themselves to each other willingly with the understanding that each one has no ownership rights to their own body. Being one flesh, your bodies belong not to you, but to your spouse. When couples get selfish, men tend to withhold finances and women tend to withhold sex. Verse 5 tells you that you should not defraud one another (meaning deliberately withholding sex) except for an agreed upon period of time to be spent in fasting and prayer. When that period is over, it is expected that sexual relations will resume. It is specifically stated that the primary reason for this is to fight off Satan because of the lack of self control. When you are in the flesh, you are easily tempted.

God's standards for the sexual relationship are very clear – one man, one woman both who are virgins. Any other sexual relationship would be considered fornication (sex outside of marriage) or adultery (sex with someone other than your spouse) both of which God hates.

Since remarriage precludes either spouse from entering into a blood covenant in a virgin state, it's important to confess the sins committed in past marriages as well as any premarital sex before the remarriage. God will forgive you and cleanse you of your sin, and then it would be wise to spiritually reestablish that virgin state. If you haven't already gotten married, use the time between now and your wedding to recommit yourselves unto the Lord. Repent from any fornication and then once married, consummate the marriage in the presence of God.

If you are already married, agree to go on a sexual fast for an agreed upon time and use the time to rededicate yourselves to the Lord and allow God to cleanse you from your past and current sins and then come together again as you read in 1st Corinthians 7. The Enemy will always use your past sins against you, so confessing them so that they can be forgiven is crucial. Satan can't use those sins against you once God has forgiven and forgotten them.

God established marriage for the benefit of a husband and a wife. He created sex to be a blessing for them. Besides being the way to procreate, sex is a way to physically and spiritually become one flesh. Where God intended sex to be a way for God, man and wife to be one in spirit, Satan has perverted sex into simply a physical act. Sex is not to be something that you do, have or get through selfish motives. It should be something special that you freely give out of love only with your spouse. Love always gives, but lust always takes.

In Ephesians 5:21 you see that in addition to being submissive to God, the husband and wife are to be submissive to each other.

Ephesians 5:15-21

"15 See then that ye walk circumspectly, not as fools, but as wise, 16 redeeming the time, because the days are evil. 17 Wherefore be ye not unwise, but understanding what the will of the Lord is. 18 And be not drunk with wine, wherein is excess; but be filled with the Spirit; 19 speaking to yourselves in psalms and hymns and spiritual songs, singing and making melody in your heart to the Lord; 20 giving thanks always for all things unto God and the Father in the name of our Lord Jesus Christ; 21 submitting yourselves one to another in the fear of God."

As the husband is submissive to Christ, the wife should be submissive to her husband. Let's look deeper into Ephesians 5.

Ephesians 5:22-33

"22 Wives, submit yourselves unto your own husbands, as unto the Lord. 23 For the husband is the head of the wife, even as Christ is the head of the church: and he is the saviour of the body. 24 Therefore as the church is subject unto Christ, so let the wives be to their own husbands in every thing. 25 Husbands, love your wives, even as Christ also loved the church, and gave himself for it; 26 that he might sanctify and cleanse it with the washing of water by the word, 27 that he might present it to himself a glorious church, not having spot, or wrinkle, or any such thing; but that it should be holy and without blemish. 28 So ought men to love their wives as their own bodies. He that loveth his wife loveth himself. 29 For no man ever yet hated his own flesh; but nourisheth and cherisheth it, even as the Lord the church: 30 for we are members of his body, of his flesh, and of his bones. 31 For this cause shall a man leave his father and mother, and shall be joined unto his wife, and they two shall be one flesh. 32 This is a great mystery: but I speak concerning Christ and the church. 33 Nevertheless, let every one of you in particular so love his wife even as himself; and the wife see that she reverence her husband."

 A husband is to love his wife as Christ loves His bride – the Church. Christ loved His bride so much that He died for her that He might sanctify her and present her without blemish. A husband is to love his wife as his own body. Being one flesh, if you do anything that harms your spouse, you are in fact hurting yourself. Again, you see that the husband/wife relationship is to be more highly valued than any relationship with your in-laws.

Finally, look at an interesting verse (Eph-5:33). Husbands are to "love" their wives and wives are to revere (respect) their husbands. Much more time will be spent on this love and respect concept in a later lesson.

With a better understanding of God's plan for marriage, you can go forward serving Him in your home and marriage. Strive for spousal agreement. One sends one thousand; two send ten thousand to flight.

BLENDED FAMILIES – DISCUSSION TOPICS – LESSON 5 – The Spousal Relationship

• Besides procreation, what is one of the most important things husbands and wives are supposed to do?

• Describe how a man's brain is like a waffle.

• Describe how a woman's brain is like a plate of spaghetti.

• Discuss God's plan for sex and which scripture explains it?

• What needs to take place in a remarriage since neither spouse will enter into the marriage in a virgin state?

• What does Ephesians 5:15:33 tell us about husbands and wives being submissive?

Chapter 6

Vertical vs. Horizontal Relationship

In this lesson you will study the difference between these two relationships and discover how your relationship with God affects your relationship with others.

1st John chapter 1 gets you started:

1st John 1:3-10

"3 that which we have seen and heard declare we unto you, that ye also may have fellowship with us: and truly our fellowship is with the Father, and with his Son Jesus Christ. 4 And these things write we unto you, that your joy may be full."

"5 This then is the message which we have heard of him, and declare unto you, that God is light, and in him is no darkness at all. 6 If we say that we have fellowship with him, and walk in darkness, we lie, and do not (say) the truth: 7 but if we walk in the light, as he is in the light, we have fellowship one with another, and the blood of Jesus Christ his Son cleanseth us from all sin."

"8 If we say that we have no sin, we deceive ourselves, and the truth is not in us. 9 If we confess our sins, he is faithful and just to forgive us our sins, and to cleanse us from all unrighteousness. 10 If we say that we have not sinned, we make him a liar, and his word is not in us."

Verses 3, 7 and 9 show you how to have a good vertical relationship with God and when that relationship is on good terms, it makes it possible to have a good relationship with others. Verses 6, 8 and 10 on the other hand, show you that when sin is in your life, it blocks your vertical relationship with God. When your relationship with God is out of alignment, it also creates problems in your relationships with family and others. The only way to restore that relationship is through the confession of sin. God is faithful to forgive you and the relationships can be restored.

The Vertical Relationship

Vertical simply means up and down. This represents your personal relationship with your Lord and Savior, Jesus Christ. This part of the lesson concentrates on ways to get better acquainted with all three members of the Holy Trinity - the Heavenly Father, Jesus Christ and the Holy Spirit.

This relationship is based on faith.

Hebrews 10:38 -

"Now the just shall live by faith: but if any man draw back, my soul shall have no pleasure in him."

Faith is believing in things you can't see.

Hebrews 11:1 -

"Now faith is the substance of things hoped for, the evidence of things not seen."

Hebrews 11:3 -

"Through faith we understand that the worlds were framed by the word of God, so that things which are seen were not made of things which do appear."

You must have faith that Jesus Christ died on the Cross for your sins and rose from the dead in three days. You are saved by Grace alone, in Christ alone, by Faith alone.

John 14:6 -

"Jesus saith unto him, I am the way, the truth, and the life: no man cometh unto the Father, but by me."

John 3:16
"For God so loved the world, that he gave his only begotten Son, that whosoever believeth in him should not perish, but have everlasting life."

The only sin that will keep you out of Heaven is the sin of unbelief. God doesn't want any of His children to perish, so He sent His Son to pay the price for all of your sins.

John 3:17-21

"17 For God sent not his Son into the world to condemn the world; but that the world through him might be saved. 18 He that believeth on him is not condemned: but he that believeth not is condemned already, because he hath not believed in the name of the only begotten Son of God. 19 And this is the condemnation, that light is come into the world, and men loved darkness rather than light, because their deeds were evil. 20 For every one that doeth evil hateth the light, neither cometh to the light, lest his deeds should be reproved. 21 But he that doeth truth cometh to the light, that his deeds may be made manifest, that they are wrought in God."

The vertical relationship can only be achieved and maintained through faith.   You are not saved by your works but rather saved to do good works. Without good works, you can't prove your faith.

<u>Matthew 5:16 -</u>

"Let your light so shine before men, that they may see your good works, and glorify your Father which is in heaven."

<u>James 2:20 -</u>

"But wilt thou know, O vain man, that faith without works is dead?"

<u>James 2:26 -</u>

"For as the body without the spirit is dead, so faith without works is dead also."

Faith is just the beginning of your vertical relationship. Building and strengthening this relationship requires prayer and fasting. Prayer enhances intimacy on three levels. It builds intimacy with the one you pray to (Father God in the name of Jesus), the one you pray with (your spouse and family) and the ones you pray for (spouse, family, friends and leaders, etc). Fasting is a time of abstaining from food, drink, sleep or sex to be more highly focused during a period of spiritual growth. In other words, you humble yourself by denying something of the flesh to glorify God, enhance your spirit, and get closer to God in your prayer life.

Look at what Jesus taught in Matthew Chapter 6 about prayer and fasting.

Jesus' Teaching on Prayer

<u>Matthew 6:5</u>
"5 And when thou prayest, thou shalt not be as the hypocrites are: for they love to pray standing in the synagogues and in the corners of the streets, that they may be seen of men. Verily I say unto you, They have their reward. 6 But thou, when thou prayest, enter into thy closet, and when thou hast shut thy door, pray to thy Father which is in secret; and thy Father which seeth in secret shall reward thee openly."

"7 But when ye pray, use not vain repetitions, as the heathen do: for they think that they shall be heard for their much speaking. 8 Be not ye therefore like unto them: for your Father knoweth what things ye have need of, before ye ask him."

9   After this manner therefore pray ye:

Our Father which art in heaven, Hallowed be thy name.

10   Thy kingdom come. Thy will be done in earth, as it is in heaven.

11   Give us this day our daily bread.

12   And forgive us our debts, as we forgive our debtors.

13   And lead us not into temptation, but deliver us from evil:

*   For thine is the kingdom, and the power, and the glory, for ever. Amen.*

14   For if ye forgive men their trespasses, your heavenly Father will also forgive you;

15   but if ye forgive not men their trespasses, neither will your Father forgive your trespasses.

Jesus' Teaching on Fasting

"16 Moreover when ye fast, be not, as the hypocrites, of a sad countenance: for they disfigure their faces, that they may appear unto men to fast. Verily I say unto you, They have their reward. 17 But thou, when thou fastest, anoint thine head, and wash thy face; 18 that thou appear not unto men to fast, but unto thy Father which is in secret: and thy Father which seeth in secret shall reward thee openly."

Strive to imitate Christ. He often got away by Himself to pray in solitude. He says "when" you pray and fast, so it is assumed that they will both be part of your ongoing relationship with Him. Don't forget to listen as well during your prayer time. The vertical relationship goes both ways.

The Horizontal Relationship

Horizontal simply means flat or level. This lesson focuses on the horizontal representing your personal relationship with your spouse. It also applies to your family and everyone else here on Earth. This part of the lesson concentrates on ways to improve the relationship with your partner-for-life in marriage.

As you learned earlier, if the vertical is out of alignment, the horizontal will be negatively impacted. So, assume for now, that the vertical is OK. There are many aspects of the vertical that translate well into the horizontal since you are to be imitating Christ.

The first and foremost is prayer. The greatest thing a husband can do is pray with and for his wife on a daily basis. This is part of being the priest of the home. It provides a spiritual covering over them and puts on the armor of God to help protect them from the Enemy.

Spend time together each day reading God's Word out loud to each other.

It's important for a husband and wife to have "date night". Get a baby-sitter for a couple of hours and get out of the house at least one night per week. This helps to establish the importance of the marital relationship being higher than the parent/child relationship (see the "Priority Pyramid" in Lesson 1).

The use of your tongue will have the greatest impact on the horizontal relationships in your life. In Ephesians 4:1-5 you find how important it is to be watchful of your speech. The tongue is like the rudder on a ship. Very small in relation to the size of the ship, but it can change the course easily and dramatically.

Ephesians 4:1-5

You are to walk as Children of Light. Any sort of uncleaness or immorality, foolish talking and jesting (using derogatory comments and then saying, "Just kidding!") should not be used by someone who is a follower of Christ. Think before you speak. Take every thought captive, or in other words, think twice – speak once.

"1 Be ye therefore followers of God, as dear children; 2 and walk in love, as Christ also hath loved us, and hath given himself for us an offering and a sacrifice to God for a sweetsmelling savor.

3 But fornication, and all uncleanness, or covetousness, let it not be once named among you, as becometh saints; 4 neither filthiness, nor foolish talking, nor jesting, which are not convenient: but rather giving of thanks. 5 For this ye know, that no whoremonger, nor unclean person, nor covetous man, who is an idolater, hath any inheritance in the kingdom of Christ and of God."

There are three basic areas of sin – the lust of the flesh, the lust of the eyes and the pride of life. Within these three, there are a multitude of things you do every day that are sinful. This lesson won't get into much detail here on all the variations. Some sins are sins of commission and some are sins of omission.

Sometimes it's the things you do and sometimes it's the things you don't do that create sin. Knowing what is right and not doing it is sin as well as knowing what is wrong and still doing it.

You've learned that when there is sin in your life, in order to be forgiven you must confess the sin to God. Unconfessed sin will be a stumbling block between you, the Lord and your spouse. Even if you think no one else knows about it, you know and God knows. Satan will use it to accuse you. There will be a buildup of guilt and when there is guilt you no longer have the freedom and joy that your salvation should be bringing to your life. Your horizontal relationships will begin to breakdown.

When a breakdown starts occurring in this relationship, one of the first things to happen is that communication ceases or changes drastically. Most people, like Adam and Eve, try to hide when they feel guilty or ashamed of something they've done. When you're trying to hide something, you tend to withdraw from the very people that love and care about you. This is Satan's plan – through shame, to get you away from the safety of the flock. Once you have distanced yourself from the safety of the Body of Christ it's much easier for Satan to devour you. This is why it is so important to confess your sins quickly and be cleansed of your unrighteousness. It allows you to restore the vertical so that you can rebuild the horizontal.

The horizontal relationship requires daily effort on your part. A good marriage doesn't just happen. "Remember, if it's to be, it's up to me!"

BLENDED FAMILIES – DISCUSSION TOPICS – LESSON 6 – Vertical vs. Horizontal Relationship

- Describe the vertical relationship.

- What is the one sin that will keep you out of Heaven?

- How do you keep the vertical relationship in good condition?

- Describe the three ways prayer develops and enhances intimacy.

- Describe the horizontal relationship.

- What is the most important thing a husband can do to develop and maintain a good horizontal relationship?

- How does the Priority Pyramid influence the vertical relationship and the horizontal relationship?

- What are the three basic areas of sin?

- How does sin impact horizontal relationships and how can you restore the relationship?

Chapter 7

Step-Parenting Skills

With blended families, a very high percentage involves bringing children of all ages into the new marriage. This lesson examines some of the blessings of being a step-parent. This lesson will focus on the positive aspects of step-parenting and the next lesson will focus more on the pitfalls. First, take a look at the book of Matthew in Chapter 1 and read about one of the most significant step-dads in the Bible.

Matthew 1:18-25 -

"18 Now the birth of Jesus Christ was on this wise: When as his mother Mary was espoused to Joseph, before they came together, she was found with child of the Holy Ghost. 19 Then Joseph her husband, being a just man, and not willing to make her a publick example, was minded to put her away privily. 20 But while he thought on these things, behold, the angel of the Lord appeared unto him in a dream, saying, Joseph, thou son of David, fear not to take unto thee Mary thy wife: for that which is conceived in her is of the Holy Ghost. 21 And she shall bring forth a son, and thou shalt call his name JESUS: for he shall save his people from their sins. 22 Now all this was done, that it might be fulfilled which was spoken of the Lord by the prophet, saying, 23 Behold, a virgin shall be with child, and shall bring forth a son, and they shall call his name Emmanuel, which being interpreted is, God with us. 24 Then Joseph being raised from sleep did as the angel of the Lord had bidden him, and took unto him his wife: 25 And knew her not till she had brought forth her firstborn son: and he called his name JESUS."

To summarize in more modern terms, Joseph was engaged to Mary but not actually married yet. Mary became pregnant with Jesus through the Holy Spirit. This created a real predicament for Joseph. He and Mary weren't married but now she was expecting and it would soon become obvious to the community. Joseph thought his only option was to divorce her, but then an angel of the Lord came to him and assured him that he should not be afraid to take Mary as his wife. Joseph then did as the angel instructed and stayed with Mary and had no relations with her until after Jesus was born. Joseph was chosen by God to be the step-father of Jesus. He and Mary went on to have several more children.

Another significant step-parent was Mordecai. He stepped up to raise Esther. Esther eventually became the Queen of the Persian Empire and risked her life to save the Jewish people from a plot to wipe them from the face of the Earth.

Esther 2:7 -

And he (Mordecai) brought up Hadassah, that is, Esther, his uncle's daughter: for she had neither father nor mother, and the maid was fair and beautiful; whom Mordecai, when her father and mother were dead, took for his own daughter.

At this point, make a distinction between being a mother or father and a mom or dad. For purposes of this lesson, a mother or father is simply the biological parent. A mom or dad is the person who chooses to love and raise their children, with the understanding that they are to be a good steward of God's children. A mom and dad realize that children are a gift from God and that they belong to Him. As parents you are to watch over them and raise them to be Godly offspring so that they can someday leave the nest and duplicate the process of raising a family.

Any time you are talking about parenting, you must always go back to the "Priority Pyramid" discussed in Chapter 1. First and foremost, the marital relationship has to have a higher priority than the parent/child relationship. It's especially important with stepparenting. Mom and Dad have to have a united front at all times where the children are concerned otherwise the children will find ways to divide and conquer. There can only be one set of rules, no matter whose kids you're raising.

There are different dynamics involved when blending families with children 12 and under and those with teen-agers. Generally speaking, in the 12 and under group, time is on your side. With the older kids, you'll have to deal with a lot more rebellion. That will be dealt with in the next lesson. If it be God's Will, you will have a few more years to be a positive influence in the children's lives. You'll have more years to love them, edify them and teach Godly principles to them.

Children are a Blessing

Since this lesson is focusing on the blessings first, look at some scriptures with the 12 and under group in mind. There are blessings from having children and there are blessings from raising Godly children.

Psalms 127:3

"Lo, children are a heritage of the LORD: and the fruit of the womb is his reward."

Proverbs 23:24 -

"The father of the righteous shall greatly rejoice: and he that begetteth a wise child shall have joy of him."

Proverbs 20:11 -

"Even a child is known by his doings, whether his work be pure, and whether it be right."

Proverbs 17:6 -

"Children's children are the crown of old men; and the glory of children are their fathers."

Proverbs 29:21 -

He that delicately bringeth up his servant from a child shall have him become his son at the length.

Teaching, Correction, Discipline and Punishment

This section focuses on the teaching, correction, discipline and the necessity of punishment of children. Proverbs has many verses that speak to a parent on how to bring up their children.

An example of teaching can involve using some event that occurs in life, good or bad, and taking the time to explain to a child how that event could have happened. Naturally, this should be done in the context of a Christian world view as this is an opportunity to teach a child about who God is and how He works.

Besides behavioral things that will keep them safe and able to function in society, teach your children how to set goals, delayed gratification (seek God's Will) and how to handle money (good stewardship). Teach them about giving, sowing and reaping.

Correction is pointing out an error in behavior when a child has already been taught the right way to behave. If the error was a mistake, it's an opportunity to show grace and mercy. Teach them to confess and ask for forgiveness. Be quick to forgive them and praise them when they react quickly to the correction.

Discipline is doing the "right thing" repetitively over a period of time to reinforce the correct behavior which is desired. Boot camp in the military is an example of discipline. In a parenting situation, discipline (or chastisement) is sometimes needed when attempts to correct a behavior are deliberately ignored. Discipline requires consequences of appropriate severity so that the original teaching is reinforced. Discipline, by its nature, requires effort. Parents have to take time and be consistent with the agreed upon consequences to "disciple" their children. Certain conditions have to be met for a specified period of time until the desired behavior becomes "natural".

Punishment is something that should be reserved for the immediate termination of a negative behavior such as when a child is throwing a tantrum. Punishment normally does not result in long-term changes in a child's behavior. Punishment over an extended period can result in even more undesirable behaviors. It's a quick and easy way to deal with a problem in the short-term, as opposed to discipline that requires time and effort over an extended period of time.

Through the following Proverbs, you can see that God intended for children to be treated the same way He treats His children. He blesses them when they are obedient and He corrects them with mercy when they disobey. You need to be diligent in speaking the Word of God to your children. You can see that you don't have to teach children to be foolish. It is something they are born with, but it can be beaten out of them. Finally, you see four Proverbs that say almost the same thing, so it must be extremely important to God. You see that you must pay attention, hear the Word of God, and do not forget the wisdom that you have been given. God desires obedience much more than he wants sacrifice.

Proverbs 22:6 -

"Train up a child in the way he should go: and when he is old, he will not depart from it"

Proverbs 22:15 -

"Foolishness is bound in the heart of a child; but the rod of correction shall drive it far from him."

Proverbs 23:13 -

"Withhold not correction from the child: for if thou beatest him with the rod, he shall not die."

Proverbs 4:1 -

Hear, ye children, the instruction of a father, and attend to know understanding.

Proverbs 5:7 -

Hear me now therefore, O ye children, and depart not from the words of my mouth.

Proverbs 7:24 -

Hearken unto me now therefore, O ye children, and attend to the words of my mouth.

Proverbs 8:32 -

Now therefore hearken unto me, O ye children: for blessed are they that keep my ways.

You should be teaching your children manners. "Please" and "Thank You" should be frequent and automatic, but today, it's almost a lost art. Teaching works best by showing your children how to do something not just telling them. They learn more from catching than just hearing. Lead by example. As Christian parents, you "should" be imitators of Christ. Your children will be imitators of you.

Develop a plan early on with your spouse about how to discipline your children so that you can be in agreement. It's vital that both spouses are on the same page in the area of correction and discipline. Let the children know you love them. Encourage them that they can do all things through Christ who strengthens them. Demonstrate your unconditional love as Christ loves you.

The next lesson discusses in more detail the consequences when bad behavior goes unchecked.

A Parent's Legacy

 As you just saw, there are short-term blessings gained from the Godly teaching of your children in fulfilling the day-to-day responsibilities of being a parent. This section looks at the more long-term blessings to you as well as your children when they have moved on with their own life and after you have been promoted to Heaven.

 One of the greatest things a person will ever hear is when they get to Heaven and hear Jesus tell them, "Well done, good and faithful servant." In addition to the promised trials and tribulations, there are also promised blessings for being a good steward. It's never wrong to do the right things.

Matthew 25:21 –

"His lord said unto him, Well done, thou good and faithful servant: thou hast been faithful over a few things, I will make thee ruler over many things: enter thou into the joy of thy lord".

Proverbs 20:7 -

"The just man walketh in his integrity: his children are blessed after him."

You are to be good stewards of what God gives you. It's all His – you just manage it for Him. Have you ever seen the bumper sticker on the back of an RV that says, "We're out spending our children's inheritance"? It sounds cute or funny on the surface, but here's what Proverbs 13 says. You can see it is important not only to leave something behind for your children, but "a good man" leaves something even for his grandchildren.

Proverbs 13:22 -

"A good man leaveth an inheritance to his children's children: and the wealth of the sinner is laid up for the just."

 A virtuous woman, you find in Proverbs 31, is blessed not only by her children but even her husband blesses her and sings her praises. Also, after children grow up and can show that they have learned their lessons well and demonstrate their wisdom you see that the parents are again blessed. Even your memory is blessed IF you have been good stewards and servants for the Lord. You will see the down side to Proverbs 10:1, 10:7 and 3:35 in the next lesson.

Proverbs 31:28 -

"Her children arise up, and call her blessed; her husband also, and he praiseth her."

Proverbs 10:1

"The Proverbs of Solomon. A wise son maketh a glad father but a foolish son is the heaviness of his mother."

Proverbs 10:7

"The memory of the just is blessed: but the name of the wicked shall rot."

Proverbs 3:35 -

"The wise shall inherit glory: but shame shall be the promotion of fools."

Once you have raised God's children, you have to give them back to Him to watch over. God will give you all tests of faith when it comes to your children. It's hard to let them go and it's even harder to see them struggle or even suffer, but once you've done your job, you have to trust God. As you've seen, if you've done a good job, your children will be a blessing not only to you but to many others. If you've been a slacker, you may well suffer even more than your children. It's important to keep the marital relationship elevated above the parent/child relationship because you are judged according to your own deeds. As parents, you can't always be responsible for the actions of your children. Eventually, they will have to answer for themselves.

BLENDED FAMILIES – DISCUSSION TOPICS – LESSON 7 – Step-Parenting Skills

- Discuss why it can be a blessing to be a step-parent. .

- Discuss the differences between teaching, correction, discipline and punishment.

- What is the best way to teach your child how to do something?

- By being a good steward, what can you look forward to hearing when you get to Heaven?

- What does Proverbs 13:22 show us about God's desire for Godly generations?

- What does Proverbs 31:28 teach us about the legacy of a virtuous women?

- What does Proverbs 10:1 teach us about the benefits of raising Godly offspring?

- What does Proverbs 3:35 teach us about your legacy?

- When the children have grown and moved on with their own lives, discuss how trials and tribulations in their lives can impact your marriage.

Chapter 8

Ruled by Yours, Mine and Ours

In the previous lesson you learned how to be a good step-parent and discovered many blessings that come through obedience. This lesson takes a look at the darker side of being a step-parent. Our prayer is that if you see yourself in any of the situations described below, that you will truly spend time with the Lord. Ask Him to help you either change from these behaviors or ask Him to heal you from the wounds you may have suffered due to divorce or the loss of a spouse. This lesson will attempt to describe situations that lead to conflict for the spouses as well as those that result in rebellion by the children.

Revisit the "Priority Pyramid" from lesson 1. Most, if not all problems that arise in a marriage can find their root cause in getting the priorities out of order. Blending two existing families puts extraordinary pressure on the order of priorities. Not only do you have to create a new one-flesh relationship between the spouses, but now you have to try to blend children of two (or more) families into a cohesive unit from day one. There are also many undesirable situations that arise when you are required to deal with an exspouse. There are too many variables to mention when it comes to blending individual children so this lesson will stick to more general issues. This lesson will be based on the assumption that Christian values were not given a high priority before blending the two families since it's highly unlikely God was where He should have been. His Will would have been for reconciliation and restoration but He is faithful to forgive your sins when you repent.

<u>Dealing with Root Causes</u>

When a blended family is created after a divorce, the root cause of the divorce rarely is truly dealt with. Instead of working out whatever the problem was according to God's Word, you often attempt to just run away from the problem. Unfortunately, you invariably bring the problem with you into the new relationship. Rather than finding out what it was and resolving it, you just try to run away and hide from it (like Adam and Eve after they had sinned). You still have possession of your original problem.

Unfortunately, you now have all sorts of additional woundedness and guilt resulting from the previous failed relationship. If the original problem(s) and the feelings of guilt and/or woundedness are not dealt with, they will most definitely impact your new relationship. Lack of forgiveness of ex-spouses always carries forward into any remarriage and brings with it negative consequences.

In most cases of divorce, there was unconfessed and unforgiven sin. When not resolved, it interferes with your vertical and horizontal relationships. Where there is sin in the camp, you cannot truly be one-flesh. It's difficult to be honest with your spouse and even more difficult to be honest with yourself. Once the one-flesh entity is being ripped apart, trust is broken. You blame everything and everyone else for your problems. You feel like you are only the victim here.

Actually being the victim of violence or abuse will be discussed later in this lesson. What does scripture tell you about being a victim of your circumstances? The following scripture from Romans clearly states that each and every one shall have to give an account of himself to God. You won't be able to blame anyone else for why you did what you did.

<u>Romans 14:12 -</u>

"So then every one of us shall give account of himself to God".

Divorce is always hardest on the children. Where God desires Godly offspring, it hurts him when his children have to suffer due to the hardness of their parents' hearts. Speaking harshly about your ex-spouse (or anyone for that matter) is never a good idea. It creates a hostile situation for the children of the failed marriage. It puts the children in a position of having to love one parent and hate the other. In order to prevent a lack of forgiveness in a previous marriage from impacting a remarriage, you'll ultimately have to do what you should have done before the divorce – forgive your former spouse.

Read the following two scriptures.

Matthew 12:36 –

"But I say unto you, That every idle word that men shall speak, they shall give account thereof in the day of judgment."

You are to control your tongue. Every word you speak will be judged by Christ.

Exodus 34:7

"keeping mercy for thousands, forgiving iniquity and transgression and sin, and that will by no means clear the guilty; visiting the iniquity of the fathers upon the children, and upon the children's children, unto the third and to the fourth generation."

When there is a sin (a lack of forgiveness for example), that sin tends to be transferred to the third and fourth generations. Generational curses generally start when a child refuses to forgive a parent for something. That child will carry that unforgiveness into their adult life and it will affect most of the decisions that they make as an adult.

Many times, your choices have the same consequences on your own children that you suffered through as a child. If you hated one of your parents for any reason and then had kids of your own, eventually you would have done something that would have hurt them.

They most likely would grow up to hate you because you would have taught them how not to forgive. Forgiveness can put an end to the generational curses.

Take a look at another common root cause of marital conflict. Selfishness is a major cause of problems in a marriage. It creates a division in the one-flesh relationship and a house divided against itself cannot stand. When you become selfish, you have just put yourself above God on the "Priority Pyramid". Selfishness manifests itself in many ways. You care more about yourself than you do about others. You are more interested in accommodating your own fleshly desires. You want what you want when you want it. You will try to hide your sins from your spouse, but God will eventually expose them. You will slip up eventually and the exposed sin will cause you much more pain than a confessed, repented and forgiven sin ever would. When a hidden sin is exposed it causes pain to your family members as well. Sin never impacts only you. It always involves others. For example – when a public figure has the sin of adultery exposed, the whole world finds out and starts judging them. This causes a great amount of embarrassment to the family even though they had nothing to do with the transgression.

Another big problem in blended families is when one spouse can't allow themselves to put the marriage and the children in the right priority according to the "Priority Pyramid". Frequently, one spouse elevates the existing relationship with their biological children above that of the marital relationship with the new spouse. This goes against Ephesians 5:33. When a husband is choosing his own kids over his wife and/or her children he is not loving her. When a wife is choosing her own kids over her husband and/or her children, she is not respecting him.

Ephesians 5:33 -

"Nevertheless let every one of you in particular so love his wife even as himself; and the wife see that she reverence her husband."

If there are children resulting from the remarriage, these children tend to be elevated above all the other children. The "Yours, Mine and Ours" situation often creates major stress on the marriage. It can be resolved by the parents accepting the fact that all the children are "Ours". Children figure out quickly where they stand in a blended family. They can tell who the favorite is. There can only be one set of rules for all the children.

When you bring children around age 12 and up, you have a much higher risk of them rebelling against you or your new spouse. Teenagers seem to be wired especially to rebel. These are the years that put the most strain on any marriage, but without a doubt can create havoc in a blended family.

If, when you get remarried, your spouse brings teenagers into your life, they will likely be the most selfish, unappreciative, uncooperative and insensitive individuals you will ever know, at least at first. It's their job to test your character and resolve. They want to see what you are made of. They want to see what makes you so special that their parent chose to marry you. If you learned anything from the previous lesson, after you have passed the tests, they should settle down and resemble normal human beings.

It's much more difficult for a spouse to become a person of authority when the kids are teens. They are already at the age where they want to rebel, and to them, you're just another person to rebel against. Getting the "Priority Pyramid" in the correct order quickly sets the stage for a positive outcome. Each spouse has to honor and respect the other as described in lesson 1 so that the kids realize that nothing they do will break up the new marriage.

In order to have any chance of survival, you and your spouse MUST quickly figure out how to agree upon the boundaries that you will need to set for the teens. As much as they hate to admit it, teens really do appreciate boundaries. They always seem to see how far they can push the limits, but when you can respond in grace and mercy but with discipline when necessary, you will eventually earn their respect. If you show any crack in your oneflesh approach to parenting, you will surely lose the battle and possibly the war.

Dealing with Abuse or Violence

A statistic that is far too high is the number of spouses and children that suffer from abuse. Many divorces are the result of abusive spouses. Children are the primary victims of abuse. It's much more difficult for them to resist the actions of an adult. This lesson can only scratch the surface of dealing with abuse but a couple of references will be provided at the end of this lesson as to where you can get resources that deal specifically with this subject.

Parents and step-parents alike are both guilty of abuse. Needless to say, God is not truly present when abuse of a spouse or child is being perpetrated. There seems to be no appreciation as to the infinite value of a spouse or a child. The most common types of abuse are physical abuse ranging from violent beatings to neglect, mental and verbal abuse and sexual abuse.

In an abusive situation, the first step should be for the victim to get away from the abuser. Obviously, this is not easy. It will take outside help in most cases. It takes finances to be able to arrange for travel to a safe place and then be able to stay there for a time. Victims have very limited access to funds. There is often no time to prepare to leave since there may be very limited opportunity. Very few places are designed for a child to go on their own to escape abuse. Therefore, they are dependent on an older sibling, a parent or other family member.

Once you've managed to get to a safe place and can feel secure with your physical surroundings, it's time to start dealing with the spiritual ramifications of the abuse. In this case you really are a victim. The natural "reaction" is to hate the abuser. However, that does not excuse you from what Jesus said above in Romans 14:12. You will ultimately be responsible for your own actions going forward.

Suffering abuse, in many cases, over a period of years, does a lot of spiritual damage. Only God can heal the wounds.

1st Peter 2:24 -

"Who his own self bare our sins in his own body on the tree, that we, being dead to sins, should live unto righteousness: by whose stripes ye were healed."

Distance from the abuser, time spent getting to know the Lord, and ultimately knowing Him well enough to trust Him and His Word, will allow you to forgive your abuser.

Forgiveness is essential because the sins of others that you do not forgive, you retain. The sin becomes yours and you will be judged accordingly. God forgives you in the same amount that you forgive those who offend you. If you do, he does. If you don't, he doesn't.

John 20:23

"Whose soever sins ye remit, they are remitted unto them; and whose soever sins ye retain, they are retained."

Matthew 6:12 -

And forgive us our debts, as we forgive our debtors.

Matthew 6:14 -

For if ye forgive men their trespasses, your heavenly Father will also forgive you:

Matthew 6:15 -

But if ye forgive not men their trespasses, neither will your Father forgive your trespasses.

In the final scripture below, Isaiah 43:25, note that God blots out your transgressions not for your sake but for His sake. When He forgives, He also forgets. This concept is hard for many people to grasp. Have you ever told someone that you could never forgive them for something they did to you? There is a feeling that if you were to forgive them for the offense, that you would be letting them "off the hook" and they would no longer be responsible for their actions.

It has already been discussed that each and every one will be accountable only for themselves on judgment day. In reality, forgiveness lets YOU off the hook. The offense will no longer be yours. You won't have to carry the burden of it any longer.

Isaiah 43:25 -

"I, even I, am He who blots out your transgressions for My own sake; And I will not remember your sins.

Like God, you should incorporate the forgetting (as much as humanly possible) as well as the forgiving.

It's one of the few acts of selfishness that is actually a good thing.

Reference material for dealing with abuse

"Vessels of Honor - Ministry to the Abused"

CURRICULUM

This booklet is a step-by-step guide to overcoming the effects of abuse, be it physical, sexual or emotional. Designed as a six week course for couples to go through together, many have found new life after going through this course. Written by Gwen and Arnold Tackett, the founders of Vessels of Honor, a ministry dedicated to the healing power of Christ to those who have suffered abuse. Gwen and Arnold are highly demanded marriage speakers across the country.

http://www.marriageamerica.biz/index.php/vessels-of-honor.html

"Picking up the Broken Pieces"

Written by Carol A. Snapp in 2008, this book was written to help a younger child of abuse get through a week. Full of pictures and easy to read for the younger readers.

Contact Carol by email at *blendedfamilies@cox.net*

This link provides access to both of these resources.

http://web.mac.com/waynejboyd/Site_3/Home.html

BLENDED FAMILIES – DISCUSSION TOPICS – LESSON 8 – Ruled by Yours, Mine and Ours

- What is one of the primary causes of dysfunction in a blended family?

- Discuss the necessity of dealing with the root cause of a problem.

- What does scripture tell us about being a victim?

- Why is it important to be watchful of your speech at all times, but especially regarding a former spouse?

- How do "curses" get passed on from one generation to another?

- What is one of the most common causes of marital conflict?

- What has to happen to truly heal the wounds of abuse?

Chapter 9

Teachable Moments vs. Discipline and Punishment

Lesson 7 discussed the basic differences between teaching, correction and discipline. This lesson takes a deeper look into the wisdom of teaching, correction and discipline and makes a distinction between discipline and punishment.

God intended for you to be obedient to His Word but gave you free will to choose between obedience and rebellion. He loved us enough to give you boundaries to keep you out of trouble. One of God's principles is "Ask, and ye shall receive". You're asking for trouble whenever you step outside those boundaries and that's what you'll receive.

Teach Your Children so They Have Wisdom and Understanding

God wants His people to be the wisest people on the planet so that others will see His Glory in them. When they see His Glory, many will repent of their sins and come to the salvation of the Lord. He wants you not only to get knowledge and know wisdom but to understand how and when to apply wisdom when you get it. As stated in Proverbs 1:7 below, the fear (or reverence) of God is the beginning of knowledge.

One of the better examples of this is the very beginning of Proverbs.

Proverbs 1:1-7 -

"1 The proverbs of Solomon the son of David, king of Israel; 2 To know wisdom and instruction; to perceive the words of understanding; 3 To receive the instruction of wisdom, justice, and judgment, and equity; 4 To give subtilty to the simple, to the young man knowledge and discretion. 5 A wise man will hear, and will increase learning; and a man of understanding shall attain unto wise counsels: 6 To understand a proverb, and the interpretation; the words of the wise, and their dark sayings. 7 The fear of the LORD is the beginning of knowledge: but fools despise wisdom and instruction."

The Old Testament gave the Hebrews "the law". There were 613 laws that the Hebrews were supposed to obey. God's intention for the law was to show people that there was no way they could be 100% righteous 100% of the time. With that knowledge, hopefully, they would have the understanding and wisdom to realize that they needed a savior. With Jesus, God's children entered into the age of Grace. Jesus fulfilled the law perfectly, innocently dying on the cross to pay the debts for the sins of the world, and rose again so that you could have everlasting life.

In the Old Testament, there are many admonitions to know the law and teach it to your children. God wants Godly offspring so the only way that's going to happen is if the parents teach the children about Him.

Look at a few Old Testament scriptures that tell us what God said about teaching from the perspective of the law.

Exodus 18:20 -

"And thou shalt teach them ordinances and laws, and shalt shew them the way wherein they must walk, and the work that they must do."

Exodus 24:12 -

"And the LORD said unto Moses, Come up to me into the mount, and be there: and I will give thee tables of stone, and a law, and commandments which I have written; that thou mayest teach them."

Leviticus 10:11 -]

"And that ye may teach the children of Israel all the statutes which the LORD hath spoken unto them by the hand of Moses."

Deuteronomy 6:7 -]

"And thou shalt teach them diligently unto thy children, and shalt talk of them when thou sittest in thine house, and when thou walkest by the way, and when thou liest down, and when thou risest up."

Jesus was constantly teaching His disciples and the throngs that followed Him. He used parables (stories) to create teachable moments for them. Here are some New Testament scriptures that show you how important teaching was to Christ.

Matthew 28:20 –

"Teaching them to observe all things whatsoever I have commanded you: and, lo, I am with you always, even unto the end of the world. Amen."

Mark 4:2 -

"And he taught them many things by parables, and said unto them in his doctrine,"

Mark 4:33 -

"And with many such parables spake he the word unto them, as they were able to hear it."

If You Love Your Children You Will Correct Them

Now, look at what God says about correction. Correction can be another form of teachable moment. Correction is necessary when your children start getting off course and get too close to the boundaries that you have previously taught them to abide by. Correction involves the next level of teaching. That level is the teaching of what the consequences will be in the future if the behavior fails to be corrected.

The first of the following three scriptures from Proverbs shows you that accepting correction is a smart thing to do. By receiving correction you become wise. It also gives you the authority to correct your own children. The second scripture below tell us that when you correct your children, later you will be able to have peace about them and they will be a delight to enjoy. The third shows you the consequences when you fail to correct your children when they are young. For those of you that despise correction, ultimately you will end up in the Lake of Fire since the Spirit of God is not in you.

Proverbs 15:5 -

"A fool despiseth his father's instruction: but he that regardeth reproof is prudent."

Proverbs 29:17 -

"Correct thy son, and he shall give thee rest; yea, he shall give delight unto thy soul."

Proverbs 15:10 -

"Correction is grievous unto him that forsaketh the way: and he that hateth reproof shall die."

These two verses from Jeremiah below give you an idea of how God corrects you. You must always understand His correction is out of love and that He is a merciful God. Only if you persist in your disobedience and lack of repentance will His wrath eventually fall upon you.

Jeremiah 10:24 -

"O LORD, correct me, but with judgment; not in thine anger, lest thou bring me to nothing."

Jeremiah 30:11 -

"For I am with thee, saith the LORD, to save thee: though I make a full end of all nations whither I have scattered thee, yet will I not make a full end of thee: but I will correct thee in measure, and will not leave thee altogether unpunished."

Discipline focuses more on positive leadership over a period of time (like boot camp for example – although some would argue whether boot camp is positive or negative). Punishment is normally something physical, quick and painful used to effect an immediate change in behavior (like spanking or slapping). In more severe instances, punishment could be used for long-term control of erroneous behavior (like prison time).

Rebellion Shows a Lack of Understanding and Leads to Punishment

Punishment comes in several different flavors. As previously mentioned, there's physical punishment such as slapping or spanking and then there are things like yelling, restricting rewards, and the penalty phase. Punishment taken to the extreme is abusive.

Do you teach and correct? Do you provide discipline through training? Or do you tend to jump directly to the punishment phase with your children? Parents that tend to punish their children often don't really understand the importance of teaching because they were punished rather than taught when they were young. Punishment is a quick and easy tool that takes far less time and patience to administer than using teaching and correction.

Teaching, correction and discipline are all ways to produce a positive end-result. Hopefully, after these three phases have been done, a child will be able to exercise selfcontrol when left alone and then also maintain it later in life. Punishment on the other hand is more of a short-term stop-gap measure that rarely results in any long-lasting change in behavior. It produces lots of resentment and bitterness towards the punisher.

Most children who are punished frequently have a very hard time understanding a loving Heavenly Father. Father God is loving, merciful and longsuffering desiring obedience over sacrifice. Only when you have hardened your heart to the point of no return, will He turn you over to your own wickedness and the consequences of your choices.

Punishment is still a form of teaching. Children quickly learn to equate love with pain. That equation gets carried forward into their adult life and if not dealt with, they end up punishing their spouse and kids in the belief they are showing love. Domestic violence is often the adult scenario when punishment was the prevailing teaching technique during childhood.

In the following scriptures, take a look at what God says about discipline (or chastisement) and punishment. Remember discipline is not supposed to be a bad thing. Punishment is for those who hate discipline.

God loves you and doesn't want any of His children to perish, so He does give you a swat on the behind occasionally when you stray too far outside the boundaries. More than anything God wants you to confess your sins and repent so that He can forgive you and restore that vertical relationship that is lost when disobedience is present.

Hebrews 12:7 -

"If ye endure chastening, God dealeth with you as with sons; for what son is he whom the father chasteneth not?"

The above gives you hope and encouragement that if you accept and endure the correction of God, He will treat you as sons/daughters.

Thankfully, you are now living in the age of Grace. What you have today is prison instead of being stoned to death as was required in the following scriptures from Deuteronomy.

Deuteronomy 21:18-23 -

"18 If a man have a stubborn and rebellious son, which will not obey the voice of his father, or the voice of his mother, and that, when they have chastened him, will not hearken unto them: 19 Then shall his father and his mother lay hold on him, and bring him out unto the elders of his city, and unto the gate of his place; 20 And they shall say unto the elders of his city, This our son is stubborn and rebellious, he will not obey our voice; he is a glutton, and a drunkard. 21 And all the men of his city shall stone him with stones, that he die: so shalt thou put evil away from among you; and all Israel shall hear, and fear."

Throughout Psalms you see that being chastened by God is truly a blessing. It reminds you that He cares enough about you to remind you of His commandments. You also see that the wicked will eventually get their "just deserts". Yes "deserts" – sometimes God will allow you to wander in the desert until you get over yourself. Also, there is nothing you do that escapes the eyes of God. He knows your heart as well as your deeds.

Psalms 94:12 -

"Blessed is the man whom thou chastenest, O LORD, and teachest him out of thy law;"

Psalms 28:4 -

"Give them according to their deeds, and according to the wickedness of their endeavours: give them after the work of their hands; render to them their desert."

Psalm 10:14

"Thou hast seen it; for thou beholdest mischief and spite, to requite it with thy hand: the poor committeth himself unto thee; thou art the helper of the fatherless."

In the following from Proverbs, note that it's not wise to punish those who do good or those in positions of responsibility who are standing uprightly. Verse 17:11 shows us that those who deliberately seek to cause trouble will face a cruel sentence when they are judged. Verse 19:25 tells us again how those who have understanding readily accept correction and even the simple-minded will learn a lesson when a fool is punished.

Proverbs 17:26

"Also to punish the just is not good, nor to strike princes for equity."

Proverbs 17:11

"An evil man seeketh only rebellion: therefore a cruel messenger shall be sent against him."

Proverbs 19:25

"Smite a scorner, and the simple will beware: and reprove one that hath understanding, and he will understand knowledge."

God's principle is that you are to confess your sins and repent. God desires restoration and reconciliation. He is faithful to forgive you but only if you forgive others. He is longsuffering and willing to let you start over. New beginnings can be fun. Tomorrow is a new day and can be your new beginning. You are a new creation in Christ Jesus. If you don't get it right the first time, begin again.

Life is full of tests. Some tests are expected, but God does have a sense of humor and will occasionally throw you a Pop Quiz. The greatest thing about one of God's tests is that it is always an OPEN BOOK test. You have all the answers you need. You just have to seek and ask for the answers. If you have trouble with any of the questions on the test, you have the ability to get 1-on-1 tutoring to help you pass the test. It doesn't' matter to God where you've been, He cares more about where you end up.

BLENDED FAMILIES – DISCUSSION TOPICS – LESSON 9 – Teachable Moments vs. Discipline and Punishment

- Why are you supposed to teach your children?

- What was God's purpose for giving his people so many laws to obey?

- What does God expect from His children?

- How does God show us that He loves us?

- Discuss the 4 phases of teaching and how they differ from one another.

- What is one of the most common results of too much punishment and not enough of the other 3 phases of teaching?

- What is the long-term benefit to teaching and correcting your children when they are young?

- Discuss what happens to those who are rebellious based on Deuteronomy 21:18-23.

Chapter 10

Forgiveness and Acts of the Spirit

This lesson digs deeper into forgiveness and then compares the fruits of the Holy Spirit with works of the flesh. Getting to know yourself from God's viewpoint is a good first step in understanding why you need to be forgiven as well as willing to forgive. Being able to look into a mirror and see what God sees will enable you to start walking down the path of change. You'll be able to start changing your behavior. Your general outlook on life will improve and the way you interact with others will bless them and you as well. The happiest people are those that have an attitude of gratitude. Through increased knowledge and understanding of what God truly says about you, the healing of old wounds can begin. There is freedom to be gained by believing God. There is bondage to be suffered by believing the lies of the Devil.

<u>Why Forgive?</u>

There are two sides to the coin of forgiveness. Heads is receiving forgiveness for sins you commit. Tails is giving forgiveness to those who sin against (or offend) you in some way. There will be many opportunities for you to flip this coin. Whichever way the coin lands, whether you need to be forgiven or you need to forgive someone else, you would be wise to be quick in doing it.

When you've committed a sin, it's a sin against God not just another person. You have just put a roadblock in the vertical relationship between you and God. The process of dealing with sin consists of being convicted by the Holy Spirit which produces a Godly sorrow for the sin. Godly sorrow is a deep recognition and understanding that you have done something to offend God. That's different than the superficial sorrow you feel when you get caught doing something wrong. You have to confess the sin to God with a sincere heartfelt attitude of repentance. God will then be faithful to forgive your sins. God forgives and makes a point to erase it from His memory. To Him, it's like it never happened. For man, it's harder to forget, but with true forgiveness, the pain will fade.

<u>Psalms 103:8-12</u>

"The LORD is merciful and gracious, slow to anger, and plenteous in mercy. 9 He will not always chide: neither will he keep his anger for ever. 10 He hath not dealt with us after our sins; nor rewarded us according to our iniquities. 11 For as the heaven is high above the earth, so great is his mercy toward them that fear him. 12 As far as the east is from the west, so far hath he removed our transgressions from us."

Most people have an easier time asking God to forgive them when it's just between them and God. It's more difficult for people to let go of things that someone else did to them. Offense is an interesting trap. When you are offended, you want to blame the offending party for "making" you feel angry or hurt. That would be fine if the other party actually had the power to do that. It's your emotion, you either control it, or it will control you. Emotion causes you to react based on how you feel without considering all the facts. When you are the Master of your emotions, you consider the situation fully and then respond based on what you know to be true.

Your normal reaction to an offense is to get even. Scripture clearly tells us that vengeance is only for the Lord to handle. Only in His control can perfect justice be applied to those who offend His children. In your humanness, you are not privy to the ultimate Will of God. That's why you need to take every thought captive, put your God Glasses on and respond as Jesus would.

Romans 12:19 -

"Dearly beloved, avenge not yourselves, but rather give place unto wrath: for it is written, Vengeance is mine; I will repay, saith the Lord."

When you encounter a situation that creates an offense against you, the Enemy now has an open door to inflict more pain and suffering. Every offense against you, when not forgiven, becomes like another brick in your backpack. An offense to you should be seen as an object that's laid at your feet. You have to make a conscious decision to either pick it up and carry it with you or just let it lay there. If you pick it up, it becomes your possession and now you own it. You are responsible for it. If you don't pick it up, you don't have to carry it around with you or make room in your daily life for it to continue to exist.

It's also something you have the option to remove from your backpack at any time to lighten your load. Adding the brick to your backpack is the same as you committing a sin in the earlier paragraph. Before you choose to feel offended, remember what Christ said on the cross in Luke 23:34. Forgiveness removes the brick from the backpack and restores the vertical relationship with God and then He can start the process of healing your wound.

Luke 23:34 –

"Then said Jesus, Father, forgive them; for they know not what they do. And they parted his raiment, and cast lots."

Forgiveness is something you do for yourself. It's not something you do for the person that committed the offense. Forgiving others is a prerequisite for having your own sins forgiven. As Matthew 6 states, you will be forgiven according to the same measure you forgive others and if you do not forgive, you will not be forgiven.

Matthew 6:12 -

"And forgive us our debts, as we forgive our debtors".

Matthew 6:14-15

"For if ye forgive men their trespasses, your heavenly Father will also forgive you: But if ye forgive not men their trespasses, neither will your Father forgive your trespasses."

Later in the book of Matthew, Jesus teaches us that there is no limit to the amount of forgiving that we must do and reinforces the fact that God will not forgive us if we do not forgive.

Matthew 18:21-35

21 Then Peter came to him and asked, "Lord, how often should I forgive someone who sins against me? Seven times?" 22 "No!" Jesus replied, "seventy times seven! 23 "For this reason, the Kingdom of Heaven can be compared to a king who decided to bring his accounts up to date with servants who had borrowed money from him. 24 In the process, one of his debtors was brought in who owed him millions of dollars. 25 He couldn't pay, so the king ordered that he, his wife, his children, and everything he had be sold to pay the debt. 26 But the man fell down before the king and begged him, 'Oh, sir, be patient with me, and I will pay it all.' 27 Then the king was filled with pity for him, and he released him and forgave his debt. 28 "But when the man left the king, he went to a fellow servant who owed him a few thousand dollars. He grabbed him by the throat and demanded instant payment. 29 His fellow servant fell down before him and begged for a little more time. 'Be patient and I will pay it,' he pleaded. 30 But his creditor wouldn't wait. He had the man arrested and jailed until the debt could be paid in full. 31 "When some of the other servants saw this, they were very upset. They went to the king and told him what had happened. 32 Then the king called in the man he had forgiven and said, 'You evil servant! I forgave you that tremendous debt because you pleaded with me. 33 Shouldn't you have mercy on your fellow servant, just as I had mercy on you?' 34 Then the angry king sent the man to prison until he had paid every penny. 35 "That's what my heavenly Father will do to you if you refuse to forgive your brothers and sisters in your heart."

In the era of grace and mercy brought to you through Jesus Christ, you have been given freedom from the laws that applied in the Old Testament (see Galatians 5:13-15). Love fulfills the law. However, God's principles still apply. Grace is the gift of salvation. Mercy keeps you from getting stoned (with rocks) every time you do something wrong. In simple terms, Grace is getting what you don't deserve and Mercy is NOT getting what you DO deserve.

Galatians 5:13-15

"13 For, brethren, ye have been called unto liberty; only use not liberty for an occasion to the flesh, but by love serve one another. 14 For all the law is fulfilled in one word, even in this; Thou shalt love thy neighbor as thyself. 15 But if ye bite and devour one another, take heed that ye be not consumed one of another."

Do You Act in the Spirit or Flesh?

Men and women have two distinct natures. You are eternal spiritual beings trying to figure out how to live a human existence. Most think the opposite – that you are human beings trying to figure out how to live a spiritual life. You WILL spend eternity somewhere. It's your choice as to where. The default is Hell, so if you don't make a conscious decision to accept Christ as your Lord and Savior, you have basically made your decision to accept the default. As you stroll through Galatians Chapter 5:16-26, you discover two distinct lists that describe each of these two natures. A table following the scriptures makes it easier to see the differences.

Galatians 5:16-26

(The Fruit of the Spirit and the Works of the Flesh)

"16 This I say then, Walk in the Spirit, and ye shall not fulfil the lust of the flesh. 17 For the flesh lusteth against the Spirit, and the Spirit against the flesh: and these are contrary the one to the other; so that ye cannot do the things that ye would. 18 But if ye be led of the Spirit, ye are not under the law."

"19 Now the works of the flesh are manifest, which are these, adultery, fornication, uncleanness, lasciviousness, 20 idolatry, witchcraft, hatred, variance, emulations, wrath, strife, seditions, heresies, 21 envyings, murders, drunkenness, revelings, and such like: of the which I tell you before, as I have also told you in time past, that they which do such things shall not inherit the kingdom of God."

"22 But the fruit of the Spirit is love, joy, peace, long-suffering, gentleness, goodness, faith, 23 meekness, temperance: against such there is no law. 24 And they that are Christ's have crucified the flesh with the affections and lusts. 25 If we live in the Spirit, let us also walk in the Spirit. 26 Let us not be desirous of vainglory, provoking one another, envying one another."

Works of the Flesh	Fruits of the Spirit
Adultery	Love
Fornication	Joy
Uncleanness	Peace
Lasciviousness	Long-suffering
Idolatry	Gentleness(Kindness)
Witchcraft(Sorcery)	Goodness
Hatred	Faith
Variance(Contentions or Quarreling)	Meekness
Emulations(Jealousies)	Temperance(Self-Control)
Wrath(anger)	
Strife(Selfish ambitions)	
Seditions(treason or dissentions)	
Heresies	
Envy	
Murder	
Drunkenness	
Revelries	
And the like	

As you can see, the works of the flesh list is about twice as long as the fruits of the Spirit. You are accountable to God for the choices you make. This list is not a menu from a Chinese restaurant. You should only be picking from Column "B", not "A". It's no wonder that there is a constant battle going on – your flesh against your spirit. Like Paul, you suffer through times when you know right from wrong, but still want to choose the works of the flesh. God is always willing and faithful to forgive these bad choices as long as you are willing and faithful to confess them.

In wrapping up this lesson, consider how valuable self-control is. You can eliminate a lot of grief, stress and heartache from your life if you can become not the Master of the Universe, but merely the Master of your own emotions.

Proverbs 16:32 -

"It is better to be patient than powerful; it is better to have self-control than to conquer a city."

BLENDED FAMILIES – DISCUSSION TOPICS – LESSON 10 – Forgiveness and Acts of the spirit

- What are two sides to the coin of forgiveness?

- Discuss the process that ultimately leads to asking for forgiveness of a sin you have committed.

- Discuss how being offended can be a trap set up by the Enemy.

- Who benefits from forgiveness and why?

- Discuss the difference between Grace and Mercy.

- Discuss the "works of the flesh" vs. the "fruits of the Spirit" in context of Proverbs 16:32.

Chapter 11

Respond in Grace - not Emotion

So what's the difference? In the last lesson you learned some of the reasons why emotion should be controlled by you instead of it controlling you. You also learned that self-control is highly valued by God. In this lesson you will gain some deeper insight into how truly significant self-control is in your journey to become Christ-like.

Some of this will probably sound very familiar by now, but that just means it's important enough to mention more than once. Emotion is not in and of itself evil or bad. It's a necessary part of your life. It's what produces the "fight or flight" ability when you get into a dangerous situation. Fear can help keep you out of trouble, but it can also paralyze you when you should be doing something constructive.

Responding in Grace

Remember from the last lesson that Grace is getting what you don't deserve. God, through His Grace, has given you many blessings that you do not deserve. As seen in the following from Luke – "to whom much is given, much is required."   One of those requirements is that you extend grace to those you meet and especially your own family.

Luke 12:48 -

But he that knew not, and did commit things worthy of stripes, shall be beaten with few stripes. For unto whomsoever much is given, of him shall be much required: and to whom men have committed much, of him they will ask the more.

The greatest blessing of all is the gift of His Son, Jesus Christ. When Christ died for your sins, you were blessed with being able to live under a new covenant of Grace instead of the old covenant of the law. Living under Grace means that you now have liberty and do not have to stay in bondage to your sins. Through Christ, you have a means of forgiveness of sin and therefore, you are no longer slaves to it but are now free.

Romans 6:14 -

For sin shall not have dominion over you: for ye are not under the law, but under grace.

Do you understand the difference between responding and reacting? Respond means to give an answer or say something in return. The implication here is that there is some degree of thought behind the answer or reply. When you respond to a question or action prompted by someone else, the expectation is that you are going to take some time to process the input before spitting back the output.

Going back to the previous lesson, remember the 'Flesh" list and the "Spirit" list.. You can also look at them as lists of possible ways to respond to any given situation. You can determine the condition of your heart based on which one of the responses you choose. When you speak, you speak out of the abundance of your heart. Be wise, and listen to yourself talk once in awhile and really hear what you sound like.

Matthew 12:34 -

"O generation of vipers, how can ye, being evil, speak good things? for out of the abundance of the heart the mouth speaketh."

The King James Version of Genesis 4:7 really doesn't translate well into today's language but other versions create a much better picture of what is being said. Below is the KJV version followed by a more modern interpretation.

Genesis 4:7 -

"If thou doest well, shalt thou not be accepted and if thou doest not well, sin lieth at the door. And unto thee shall be his desire, and thou shalt rule over him."

In other words, if you respond to a situation in the right way (God's way), you will be accepted by Him and other men. But if you do not respond correctly, then you will be in sin and the Devil will be waiting to attack and destroy you, so you are to rule over the enemy.

Paul, in his letter to the church in Corinth, tells them in verse 12, how to respond when it seems like the whole world is against you.

1 Corinthians 4:7-13 -

7 For who maketh thee to differ from another? and what hast thou that thou didst not receive? now if thou didst receive it, why dost thou glory, as if thou hadst not received it? 8 Now ye are full, now ye are rich, ye have reigned as kings without us: and I would to God ye did reign, that we also might reign with you. 9 For I think that God hath set forth us the apostles last, as it were appointed to death: for we are made a spectacle unto the world, and to angels, and to men. 10 We are fools for Christ's sake, but ye are wise in Christ; we are weak, but ye are strong; ye are honourable, but we are despised. 11 Even unto this present hour we both hunger, and thirst, and are naked, and are buffeted, and have no certain dwellingplace; 12 And labour, working with our own hands: being reviled, we bless; being persecuted, we suffer it: 13 Being defamed, we intreat: we are made as the filth of the world, and are the offscouring of all things unto this day.

Again, paraphrasing with more up-to-date language here's what Paul is communicating in the above verses from 1st Corinthians 4:7-13.

What makes you think you're so special? What do you have that you didn't receive from God? If it was given to you, why do you make it seem like you earned it on your own? Your pride is making you believe you are rich like kings and don't need anything else. Paul is telling the Corinthians that he wishes they really were kings because then he would be with them in Heaven. At times, Paul feels like a POW being paraded through a city only to be executed at the end of the march, being put on display and being made a spectacle to the whole world and even the angels. The apostles are looked at as fools by the world but when they are weak, Christ is strong. The apostles endured many hardships yet even though the world treats them like trash; they respond patiently and kindly and bless them that curse them.

The point being made in the above passage of scripture is that even when you are hated, despised, cursed and beaten God expects his children to 'respond" in Grace, with humility and a lowliness of spirit. Vengeance is His and He will judge those who do evil. You are not to respond in anger, but turn the other cheek.

Matthew 5:39 -

"But I say unto you, That ye resist not evil: but whosoever shall smite thee on thy right cheek, turn to him the other also."

It's the Holy Spirit living in you that allows you to respond that way. If Christ is not in you, you will not have the power to do it in your own flesh.

You can get a glimpse of that in the following verse from Acts.

Acts 16:14 -

"And a certain woman named Lydia, a seller of purple, of the city of Thyatira, which worshipped God, heard us: whose heart the Lord opened, that she attended unto the things which were spoken of Paul."

In this verse, the word "attended" can also be interpreted "responded". You can see that the Lord had prepared her heart to receive the Word of God that Paul spoke to her and she responded by believing.

Perhaps one of the greatest examples of responding in grace is found in Genesis chapters 37-48. Joseph, the 11th son of Jacob was sold into slavery by his own brothers. He had every reason to be offended by them. Joseph gave his best efforts when he had the chance and spent time in prison after being falsely accused of rape. He had many opportunities to be offended and carry a grudge. Yet, after all that, he was faithful to God and God blessed him, raising him up to the second highest position in Egypt after Pharaoh himself. When a famine fell upon the land, it was so bad that his brothers had to travel to Egypt to get some food. There, they unknowingly met up with Joseph and when he told them who he was, they were afraid he would kill them. Joseph extended grace and mercy to them even though they had done such an evil thing to him. Through all of his trials he came to the realization that what his brothers had intended for evil, God had a good purpose for and in it He would be glorified.

Reacting from Emotion

Emotions are feelings. Reacting is making decisions based on your feelings without regard to the facts. Responding is making decisions based on what you know to be true. There are many definitions available for the word "react", but if you break it down to its most basic form, it simply means "act again".

From that, it's relatively easy to see that when you "react" from your emotions you are most likely going to return to someone what they just did to you. If it is offensive and your emotions are in charge, you will 'act again" in the same way back to them. Reacting carries with it the implication that there is very little, if any, time taken to process or think about the impact of your response.

When a doctor taps your knee with the little rubber hammer, you experience that "knee jerk" reaction called a "reflex response". You have absolutely no mental control over whether your knee reacts to the hammer or not. You have no choice. The reflex response takes over and your leg jumps without you even thinking about it.

This example correlates directly to what people do when they are slaves to their emotions. Your emotions, in conjunction with your fallen nature, take advantage of the reflex response. When something happens that you're not prepared for, especially if you find it offensive, your emotions will trigger that reflex response. You have no plan of action; therefore you react not to the situation but to the offense. When you exercise self-control you will respond with knowledge, understanding and wisdom.

How many times do you hear someone make the excuse that, "I just couldn't help myself."? Some of you may be old enough to remember Flip Wilson. He had a TV Comedy show back in the early 1970's. One of his famous phrases was "The Devil made me do it." People in general are very quick to blame the Devil for their own misdeeds.

The Devil can only be in one place at a time and in your fallen nature, he doesn't really have to work that hard on you. You're wicked enough on your own – you don't really need his help to commit sin.

Genesis 6:5 -

"And GOD saw that the wickedness of man was great in the earth, and that every imagination of the thoughts of his heart was only evil continually."

Blame is part of the original sin in the Garden of Eden. Adam tried to blame his disobedience on God Himself for the first occurrence of sin (see Gen 3:12 below). It's your fallen nature that persistently drives you to try to offload responsibility and accountability for your own actions. Any time, and any way, that you can point the finger of blame at someone else, you tend to want to make it your first choice.

Genesis 3:12 -

"And the man said, The woman whom thou gavest to be with me, she gave me of the tree, and I did eat."

Perhaps one of the most difficult things about being a Christian is having the faith to trust the Lord when things are tough and having the resolve to not return evil for evil.

Romans 12:17 is very clear on the subject of returning evil for evil.

Romans 12:17 -

"Recompense to no man evil for evil. Provide things honest in the sight of all men."

Looking at this verse in context, you see much more from Paul as to how a follower of Christ is to be at peace with others.

Romans 12:14:21 -

"14 Bless them which persecute you: bless, and curse not. 15 Rejoice with them that do rejoice, and weep with them that weep. 16 Be of the same mind one toward another. Mind not high things, but condescend to men of low estate. Be not wise in your own conceits. 17 Recompense to no man evil for evil. Provide things honest in the sight of all men. 18 If it be possible, as much as lieth in you, live peaceably with all men. 19 Dearly beloved, avenge not yourselves, but rather give place unto wrath: for it is written, Vengeance is mine; I will repay, saith the Lord. 20 Therefore if thine enemy hunger, feed him; if he thirst, give him drink: for in so doing thou shalt heap coals of fire on his head. 21 Be not overcome of evil, but overcome evil with good."

Some years ago there was a popular bumper sticker that only had the letters "WWJD" on it. It's very simple, but it can be a great reminder to tickle your brain when you're confronted with a difficult situation. Ask yourself, "What Would Jesus Do?" Scripture teaches to take every thought captive and process it against the Word of God before you act on it. An even better question is, "What Did Jesus Do?"

2 Corinthians 10: 5

"Casting down imaginations, and every high thing that exalteth itself against the knowledge of God, and bringing into captivity every thought to the obedience of Christ;"

Hopefully by now, you're starting to get the picture. It is better to respond than to react. One last scripture to drive home this point is the following from Ephesians.

Ephesians 4:31 -

"Let all bitterness, and wrath, and anger, and clamour, and evil speaking, be put away from you, with all malice:"

As Christians, we are commanded to *"love thy neighbor as thyself"*. By loving one another, we are fulfilling the law. Consider that you first have to love yourself. You can't give what you don't have. You love God, because He *first loved you and because you know you are loved, you can give love to others. You sow, and then you reap. To receive, you must first give.*

Romans 13:8 -

"Owe no man any thing, but to love one another: for he that loveth another hath fulfilled the law."

Romans 13:10 -

"Love worketh no ill to his neighbour: therefore love is the fulfilling of the law".

Galatians 5:14 -

"For all the law is fulfilled in one word, even in this; Thou shalt love thy neighbour as thyself."

Jas 2:8 -

"If ye fulfil the royal law according to the scripture, Thou shalt love thy neighbour as thyself, ye do well:"

BLENDED FAMILIES – DISCUSSION TOPICS – LESSON 11 – Respond in Grace – not Emotion

- Why are you instructed to respond in Grace (refer to Luke 12:48)?

- Discuss the difference between the covenants in the Old and New Testaments.

- Under the covenant of Grace, what allows us to fulfill the law and how is it accomplished?

- Discuss the difference between reacting and responding to a situation.

- What does scripture tell you about how to respond to your enemies?

- Discuss the principle outlined in 2 Corinthians 10:5 that tells us to "take every thought captive" and how that helps us respond rather than react.

Chapter 12

To Earn Respect - Give Respect

Surely, you have heard the Golden Rule – "Do Unto Others as You Would Have Them Do Unto You". Have you ever wondered where it came from? Two very similar examples from scripture are found in the Gospels of Matthew and Luke.

Matthew 7:12 -

"Therefore all things whatsoever ye would that men should do to you, do ye even so to them: for this is the law and the prophets."

Luke 6:31 -

"And as ye would that men should do to you, do ye also to them likewise."

If both spouses in a marriage would only abide by this one principle, divorce would be almost non-existent. One reason the divorce rate is so high is selfishness. Men and women just don't know what the other truly needs or how to meet those needs. Selfishness takes root and due to the lack of understanding of your spouse's differences, you choose to satisfy your own needs instead. Rather than trying to figure out how best to serve the other, it's just easier to leave.

What is Respect?

Wikipedia defines respect as "the esteem for, or a sense of the worth or excellence of, a person, a personal quality, ability, or a manifestation of a personal quality or ability. In certain ways, respect manifests itself as a kind of ethic or principle, such as in the commonly taught concept of "[having] respect for others" or the ethic of reciprocity."

As a group, the parents of children born during the "Me" generation, (1970 through 1999) failed to teach their children how to serve others. It was a time when parents wanted to "give" their children all the things they never had. The children learned that all they had to do was ask and they would receive. It didn't matter to the parents if it was a need or a want. In a lot of cases, it was a want. "Ask and ye shall receive" is a Biblical principle, but the parents weren't teaching the respect and authority of God, which lead to a major decline in the children respecting anyone in or anything to do with authority. They also lost respect for themselves. Without being able respect yourself, how do you expect to be able to respect anyone else?

In a blended family especially, there is a huge need for a husband and wife to be good servants toward each other. Besides being the Christ-like thing to do, it provides a great example of love and respect for the children to observe and imitate.

Men and women are so different, it's no wonder you don't really understand the other. You are physically, mentally and emotionally different. How many of you actually take the time to learn about and appreciate these differences in your spouse? Differences should be appreciated, not despised or feared. Like you read in a previous lesson, "Different isn't wrong, it's just different". Respect the fact that God made each and every one of you unique. You have your own special purpose for being created and it's your job to get to know God intimately enough to discover what your purpose is. He will be faithful to reveal it to you.

Psalms 139:14 –

"I will praise thee; for I am fearfully and wonderfully made: marvellous are thy works; and that my soul knoweth right well."

Just as God meets all your needs, he doesn't always give you all your wants. You might want a luxury vehicle, but you might only need a bicycle to get somewhere. God will make sure you have the bicycle. In any marriage, love and respect go hand-in-hand. Men need respect. Women need love.

Read the following verse from Ephesians 5:33 below. You are told to do the opposite for your spouse than what you need for yourself. Women instinctively know and understand love. That's part of being created to be relational. Part of the curse on Eve in the Garden of Eden created a legacy for women to not want to respect their husband. Men instinctively know and understand respect. Adam's first instinct was to shift blame to his wife when God found them hiding due to the sin they had committed. That shows that his first thought was not to give himself up for his wife out of love for her.

Ephesians 5:33 -

"Nevertheless let every one of you in particular so love his wife even as himself; and the wife see that she reverence her husband."

Love and respect are two critical aspects of a healthy relationship. They're like twins, but not identical twins. It's hard to have one without the other. The relationship will suffer if either one is absent. If they were identical, the scripture would probably have been written that husbands and wives should simply love one another.

Men need and understand respect. Men would rather hear that they are respected than that they are loved. A wife can say, "I love you." all day long, but it the husband feels disrespected in any way, he won't appreciate the fact that he is loved. Few men honestly understand how to love. When a husband is asked if he loves his wife, he'll make the statement, "I married her didn't I? I told her I loved her then and if that ever changes, I'll let her know." It's a lot easier for a husband to respect his wife than love her, but that's not what she "needs". She would much rather hear from her husband, "I love you." than "I respect you."

Men generally have a desire or a hope that when they get married, their wife won't change. This stems from the fact that they feel they got what they wanted and they really don't like change. Conversely, women seem to have the notion that they will be able to correct all the faults in their husband AFTER they get married. For some reason, women always seem to change and husbands never do. You each spend a lot of time trying to change the other when you should be asking God to change YOU. God is not in the spouse changing business, He's in the YOU changing business.

Women understand and need love. When either spouse is not getting what they need, they start holding back on what the other spouse needs. When the wife perceives a lack of love from her husband, she will instinctively start withdrawing respect. Once he starts feeling that she doesn't respect him, he instinctively starts withdrawing love. Welcome to one of the most frequently ridden Merry-Go-Rounds in marriage. This is one of those rides that everyone that has ever been married has ridden. The hard part is getting off the ride. The first one that can humble themselves and say, "I'm sorry" gets the prize. Don't let pride get the best of you.

Respect is the perception of being honored or having the esteem of others. However, it's not good to think too highly of yourself. Leave that for someone else to do.

Romans 11:25 -

"For I would not, brethren, that ye should be ignorant of this mystery, lest ye should be wise in your own conceits; that blindness in part is happened to Israel, until the fulness of the Gentiles be come in."

So, how do you earn respect?

When it comes to respect, the only true way to get it is to earn it. It's not something you can demand. A dictator demands respect and uses fear tactics to get what he wants. What he really gets is obedience, not true respect. God wants obedience too, but He uses love to get what He wants. Respect comes through loving and respecting others. If you want to earn respect, you have to show respect to others. Again, you reap what you sow. You have to first give what you want in order to get what you want.

In a blended family, with children from different marriages, you can't just start demanding that the children from the other spouse respect you. You are going to have to work diligently to earn it. More often than not, there is going to be rebellion from at least one child who is more closely tied to the ex-spouse of the one you are now married to.

It's important to develop a plan of attack with your new spouse as to how you are going to parent the children. Preferably, you will do this before you actually get married. As it's been stated before, you have to have agreement and a united front when it comes to the children. As a husband trying to lead a new flock of sheep, you can't afford to let any of them get too far away from you. Your immediate job is to earn the respect of your new wife. It will speed up the process of earning the respect of the children. Once the children see that you love her and she respects you, they will begin to understand their place in the family – which is that they are in second place to the marriage.

It's going to take effort, patience and consistency on your part as the new father to be able to earn the respect of "her" kids. One way to prove yourself, is to discuss marriage goals, family goals and individual goals with and for each member of the family. As the new leader of the family, WHEN you are able to consistently meet the goals that you and your family have agreed to, and you help the children meet their goals, you will earn the respect you will need to guide your new family.

Gathering the family together and discussing what you want to accomplish for the year says a lot to the children. Finding and cutting pictures out of magazines (or printing them off the internet) to represent the chosen goals is a great way to make the goals more real to everyone. Putting those pictures on the refrigerator keeps the goals fresh in your mind. As you achieve a goal, take the picture down.

A man's word is to be his bond. If you want respect, you need to do what you say you are going to do. In Old Testament times, when a couple was to be married, it was expected that both bride and groom would be virgins when they were married. Immediately after the wedding ceremony, the bride and groom would be ushered off to a tent where they would be expected to consummate the marriage.

After some time, the two fathers would enter the tent together to check the bed linens for signs of blood. If there was no sign, it would be considered physical proof that the bride was not a virgin. The father of the bride would then have to reimburse the father of the groom for the wedding expenses. So, how do you prove that the groom was a virgin? It was expected that his word would be his bond and he would not lie about such things. Yes, it's a double standard, but it shows the importance of a man's word being something you can trust.

The currency of a man is his word. If you make promises and then don't keep them, your currency is quickly losing its value. It this becomes a habit, after awhile, your currency will be worthless. The more you do of what you say you will do, the greater will be the value of your word. Your wife is the bank that determines how much your currency is worth. She can love you in spite of what you do, but her respect for you will be based primarily on your word and your actions being equal.

Read the 1st and 5th of the Ten Commandments below from Exodus. You are to teach your children to respect God and to respect their father and mother. Showing them that you do is the best way to teach them.

Exodus 20:1-3 -

"1 And God spake all these words, saying, 2 I am the LORD thy God, which have brought thee out of the land of Egypt, out of the house of bondage.

3 Thou shalt have no other gods before me."   *(1st Commandment)*

Exodus 20:12 -

"Honour thy father and thy mother: that thy days may be long upon the land which the LORD thy God giveth thee."   *(5th Commandment)*

In addition to teaching your children about respect for God and their parents, teach them to respect the elderly. Teach them not to be afraid of the elderly, but let them know that there is much wisdom to be gleaned from them. They have many stories to tell. Suggest they volunteer in nursing homes for example. They will learn many lessons about life. Maybe they will gain a new respect for life and start taking advantage of their youth for the Glory of God.

Leviticus 19:32 -

"Thou shalt rise up before the hoary head, and honour the face of the old man, and fear thy God: I am the LORD."

Proverbs 16:31 -

"The hoary head is a crown of glory, if it be found in the way of righteousness."

Proverbs 20:29 -

"The glory of young men is their strength: and the beauty of old men is the gray head."

In Closing

We pray this curriculum has helped you understand how to put a blended family together in a way that will bring glory to God and peace to you and your spouse.   We pray that you now have more understanding about God's order for creating a Godly marriage and family. We pray that as you start applying the principles outlined in this teaching, God will pour out His blessings on your new or renewed covenant with Him.

Once again, we want to ask you the question requiring the most important answer of your life. If you were to die today, where would you end up? If you do not know absolutely, beyond a shadow of a doubt that you are 100% sure you would spend eternity in Heaven with Jesus, now is the time to make sure.

Salvation is a gift from God. You can't earn it. You have to receive it in faith that it is yours and yours alone. Like a birthday or Christmas gift with your name on it, it's not really yours until you accept the box, open it and take out the gift. Just because you know someone with a similar gift, it doesn't benefit you in any way.

Father God so loved the world that he gave His only begotten son, Jesus Christ to be the sacrifice for the sins of the world. Jesus is the only way to spend eternity in the presence of God.

<u>John 3:16 -</u>

"For God so loved the world, that he gave his only begotten Son, that whosoever believeth in him should not perish, but have everlasting life."

<u>John 14:6 -</u>

"Jesus saith unto him, I am the way, the truth, and the life: no man cometh unto the Father, but by me."

If you're ready to accept Jesus as your savior you will need to confess your sins and by faith accept His promise to forgive those sins. Then you will need to ask Him to become your Lord and Savior. The following prayer, said out loud, will gain you entrance into the Kingdom of God. You will then become a son or daughter of the King of Kings. Praise the Lord, Amen.

"Dear Heavenly Father, I confess that I have sinned against You. My sins have separated me from You. I am truly sorry, and now I want to repent from my past sinful life toward You. Please forgive me. Father, I believe that your son, Jesus Christ died on a cross for my sins and was resurrected from the dead in three days. He is alive, and He hears my prayers. I'm asking You, Jesus, to become the Lord of my life. Please rule and reign in my heart from this day forward. I am a new creation in You. Please send your Holy Spirit to help me obey You, and to do Your will for the rest of my life. In Jesus' name I pray, Amen."

BLENDED FAMILIES – DISCUSSION TOPICS – LESSON 12 – To Earn Respect – Give Respect

- What is the "Golden Rule" and where does it come from?

- Why should husbands and wives be good servants towards each other?

- Discuss Ephesians 5:33 as it relates to your natural flesh vs. spirit behaviors.

- Discuss Ephesians 5:33 as it relates to the necessity to have love and respect in a marital relationship.

- How can a husband earn respect from his "new family"?

About the Authors

Larry and Carol Snapp have been married since December, 1979. When they got married, they created a blended family. Carol had been married before and had stepchildren and knows what the term, "Yours, Mine and Ours" means. Larry had never married before. Larry inherited 3 children that Carol had from her two previous marriages.

After 23 years of marriage, there was a major crisis they had to deal with. God, through a long-time friend, introduced them to the NAME marriage ministry. He brought them together with an awesome couple that reintroduced Jesus into their life. With God's help, they were restored and after several years of counseling others that were struggling in their marriages, God gave them a vision for this teaching.

Through their own experiences they learned many good ways and wrong ways to do things. Ultimately, they learned the Godly way to do things. They had to walk through many months of trials and tribulations first hand to gain the understanding for this teaching.

Through all the testing, God put a desire in their hearts to put family values back into homes. By reaching out to one family, one man, one woman, or even one child at a time they hope to teach them God's plan for marriage. As one is taught, they in turn are able to teach others in their family or their friend's family. Their vision is to have this spread like a virus worldwide. Instead of a virus that makes you sick, this virus will heal you, your marriage and your family.

Larry and Carol are committed to God's work of rebuilding His image in hearts and minds – one family at a time.

Hopefully, God will touch your heart and you will be infected by this virus and join them in their work.

To Contact:

Email - blendedfamilies@cox.net

Web - www.theblendedfamily.net

www.ingramcontent.com/pod-product-compliance
Lightning Source LLC
Chambersburg PA
CBHW041152120626
46547CB00020B/3192